STUDIES IN HISTORY, ECONOMICS AND PUBLIC LAW

Edited by the

**FACULTY OF POLITICAL SCIENCE
OF COLUMBIA UNIVERSITY**

NUMBER 362

SIEYES: HIS LIFE AND HIS NATIONALISM

BY

GLYNDON G. VAN DEUSEN

SIEYES: HIS LIFE AND HIS NATIONALISM

BY

GLYNDON G. VAN DEUSEN

AMS PRESS

NEW YORK

COLUMBIA UNIVERSITY
STUDIES IN THE
SOCIAL SCIENCES

362

The series was formerly known as
Studies in History, Economics and Public Law.

Reprinted with the permission of Columbia University Press
From the edition of 1932, New York
First AMS EDITION published 1969
Manufactured in the United States of America

Second printing 1970

Library of Congress Catalog Card Number: 68-58632
International Standard Book Number:
    Complete Set: 0-404-51000-0
    Number 362:0-404-51362-X

AMS PRESS, INC.
New York, N.Y. 10003

PREFACE

ANY study connected with the French Revolution is bound to be interesting for the one who undertakes it, if not for those whose lot it is to scan the results. The tremendous drama of that great movement, its swift succession of events, where tragedy and comedy so intermingled, these alone make it fascinating. There is more than this for the student or lover of history. The Revolution saw the end of an old order; its evangels heralded the coming of a new. Social and political inequality, time-honored forms of government, the conservative point of view that is the inevitable accompaniment of long stabilized institutions, all these were rocked to their foundations by the all-compelling advance of liberty, equality, and fraternity.

One of the modern developments directly stimulated by this great upheaval is nationalism, and a main part of the following biography of Sieyes concerns his nationalist tendencies. I have not attempted to picture him as a full-fledged, extreme nationalist; that he was not. And in this study of his career I have sought carefully to avoid a biased viewpoint, or any exaggeration or distortion of facts and situations that would lead to false conclusions. Such a course is hard to hold, and nationalism itself, like all the great forces which motivate mankind, offers peculiar difficulties of definition. But, whether this attempt has been a success or a failure, I have at least tried to follow in the footsteps of Ranke and present the life and aims of Sieyes as they really were.

This book owes much of whatever merit it possesses to the helpful criticisms and suggestions of Professor Carlton J. H.

5

Hayes of Columbia University, to the very willing coöperation of the library staffs at Columbia and Cornell Universities, and to the courtesy of the officials in charge of the French archives that were utilized, particularly the *Archives des Affaires Etrangères* and the *Archives Nationales.*

TABLE OF CONTENTS

7

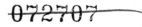

CHAPTER V

NATIONALISM. SIEYES' CONCEPTION OF FRANCE

CHAPTER VI

NATIONALISM. FURTHER PLANS FOR UNITY. DEVOTION TO LA PATRIE

CHAPTER VII

NATIONALISM. FOREIGN POLICY

CHAPTER VIII

THE FINAL YEARS. AN APPRECIATION

CHAPTER I

The Early Years

Emmanuel Joseph Sieyes [1] lived in an age of storm and stress. France passed from under an old established order to revolution, to dictatorship, to restoration, to another revolution and change of government, during his eighty-eight years, and he himself took a prominent part in various phases of that great upheaval which overthrew the Bourbons and spread the gospel of liberty, fraternity and equality throughout Europe.

The boy, fifth child of Honoré and Anne Sieyes, was born at Fréjus, in southern France, 3 March, 1748. His parents were commoners, with some tincture of noble blood in their veins, and were of moderate means, the father having a small, independent revenue, and a modest income as a local tax collector. [2]

[1] So far as I can ascertain, accentuation is optional. At the Collège des Grassins in 1769 he signed the roll as Sieyes, and this was his signature under the Directory in 1798-1799. He signed the Tennis Court oath, Siéyes, and this was his signature while on the Committee of Public Safety. A facsimile of a letter, dated 22 January, 1810, gives Sièyes. I have nowhere seen the version used by Mathiez—Sieys. *Cf.* Bibliothèque de la Ville de Paris, N. A. 191, fol. 113, and *Iconographie des contemporains*, Delpech, F. S., ed., vol. ii, no pagination. According to Camille Desmoulins, the name was pronounced Syess. *Cf.* Camille Desmoulins, *Oeuvres*, vol. ii, p. 315, Camille to his father, 3 June, 1789, and *L'Intermédiaire des chercheurs et curieux*, vol. xlvii, cols. 246-248 (20 Feb., 1903).

[2] *Notice sur la vie de Sieyes*, pp. 9-10; Teissier, O., "La Jeunesse de l'Abbé Sieyes," in *La Nouvelle Revue*, vol. 109, p. 128 (1897); Neton, A., "Les Debuts de Sieyes," in *La Nouvelle Revue*, n. s. vol. i, pp. 576-588 (1899). These two articles are the only sources for the early correspondence of Sieyes. I have made every effort to find the originals, but without success.

Emmanuel Joseph was given lessons by a tutor and by the Jesuits, and spent some time at the *collège* of the *Doctrinaires*[3] of Draguignan.   He wanted to be a soldier, but his health was feeble, his parents pious, and they favored a religious career, aid for which was offered by Césarges, the vicar-general of Fréjus, who considered himself under obligations to Honoré Sieyes.   The result was a ten-years' sojourn, 1762-1772, at the seminary of Saint Sulpice in Paris, studying philosophy and theology in preparation for the priesthood.[4]   There he made a name for himself as an able student with a special taste for the sciences and the " new philosophic principles," and no taste at all for conservative theology.[5]   The seedling was not suited to the soil and in after years Sieyes spoke of the religious instruction of this period with bitterness and disgust.   He left without a degree but continued, probably because opportunity beckoned that way, his ecclesiastical career.[6]

Sieyes was ordained priest in 1773 but preferment did not come immediately.   The young ecclesiastic felt the pinch of straitened circumstances, but he devoted himself assiduously to cultivating music and making philosophical researches,[7] pursuits for which he had plenty of time.   On 20 October, 1774, as a result of requests made by influential friends at

---

[3] Or, *Prêtres seculiers de la doctrine chrétienne*, a French religious order founded by César de Bus in 1592.

[4] *Notice*, pp. 9-11 ; Teissier, *op. cit.*, pp. 129-130, for correspondence between Césarges and the elder Sieyes, who had lent him a considerable amount of money.

[5] Teissier, *op. cit.*, pp. 130-131, letters from Césarges to H. Sieyes; Neton, *op. cit.*, p. 578, same to same ; Sainte-Beuve, " Sieyes " in *Causeries de lundi*, vol. v, p. 191.   This last is a masterly and extremely valuable essay, based on MSS. collected by M. Fortoul which have long since disappeared.

[6] *Notice*, pp. 9-12, 16-18; Sainte-Beuve, *op. cit.*, vol. v, p. 191.

[7] *Notice*, p. 14; Teissier, *op. cit.*, pp. 131-133, M. de Besplas to H. Sieyes, 26 April, 1774.

the time of the accession of Louis XVI, he obtained the promise of a canonry in Brittany, but this honor would have no pecuniary advantages attached to it until the death of the incumbent. It was not until the end of 1775 that he received his first real employment, that of secretary to M. de Lubersac, bishop of Treguier. Here he spent nearly two years and here, as deputy of the diocese, he sat in the Estates of Brittany and saw with a profound distaste the sway of the privileged classes.[8]

In 1780 Lubersac was transferred to the diocese of Chartres,[9] and Sieyes accompanied him as his vicar general, becoming in the course of time a canon of the cathedral and chancellor of the diocese.[10] He was on a commission, which, much to the disgust of his more staid associates, changed the old liturgy to the Parisian form,[11] and, no doubt because of the high favor in which he was held by Lubersac, he acted as the representative of his diocese in the Upper Chamber of the Clergy. In this capacity he lived at Paris, enjoying the high esteem of his Order because of his administrative ability, and pursuing there his philosophical studies.[12]

[8] *Ibid.*, pp. 134-135; Neton, *op. cit.*, pp. 579-580; Sainte-Beuve, *op. cit.*, vol. v, p. 201; *Notice*, p. 15, "... rien n'égale l'indignation qu'il avoit rapportée de cette assemblé, contre la honteuse oppression où la noblesse y tenoit le malheureux Tiers-État."
Césarges had obtained the secretarial position for Sieyes.

[9] Bethouart, A., *Histoire de Chartres*, vol. i, p. 17. Lubersac came to Chartres as bishop 8 August, 1780.

[10] *Archives d'Eure et Loir*, C 1, Départemental Assembly of Chartres and Dourdan, first session, 8 August, 1787; G 295, *Registre*, pp. 224, 231, years 1783, 1788, for the canonical appointment; G 336, folios 109-110, 9 April, 1788, for appointment as chancellor. The records at Chartres are distressingly scanty. M. Jusselin, the local archivist, told me that many were destroyed during the Revolution.

[11] See the plaint of a contemporary canon, Jean Vaudon, quoted by Boislaigue, R. *Le Silencieux Sieyes*, p. 20.

[12] His advancement was proof of his ability and popularity. Sir Samuel Romilly recorded in his *Life*, vol. ii, pp. 77-78, "I met the Abbé

What characteristics, what auguries of his future, were manifest in those early years before his rise to fame? Plain and almost severe in appearance,[13] his slight frame and his rather arrogantly intellectual face, with its well-defined nose and chin, large black eyes, high forehead, and pale complexion, must have given him the appearance of a scholar rather than that of a man of the beau monde. His health was poor, his eyes especially giving him much trouble,[14] and his low voice and lack of rhetorical powers put him at a disadvantage on the rostrum.[15]

Sieyes several times at the Bishop of Chartres [in Paris, autumn of 1789]; he was the Bishop's aumônier [almoner], and a person of whose talents he entertained the highest opinion." See also Sainte-Beuve, *op. cit.*, vol. v, p. 201.

[13] *Moniteur*, 7 June, 1797. Sieyes at the trial of Poule (his would-be assassin) "La nature m'a déjà donné une phisionomie assez sévère."

For portraits see the *Collection générale des portraits de MM. les députés au États généraux*, and the *Collection complète des portraits* (Bibl. Nat. Le 25.1, and Le 25.2). For later portraits, see that painted by David in 1817 (David, J., *Le peintre Louis David*, vol. 1), a good reproduction, and the one signed Maurin, 1825, in the *Iconographie des contemporains* (Delpech, F. S., ed.), vol. i.

[14] "Notice de M. Fortoul," followed by Sainte-Beuve, *op. cit.*, vol. v, p. 191; *cf.* the report of Meyer, a traveler, in Aulard, *Orateurs de la Convention*, vol. ii, pp. 555-556; and the reference to 'sa teint pale' by Talleyrand, *Memoires*, vol. ii, p. 212. For particular references to his health, see his letters to his father as published by Teissier, *op. cit.*, *passim*. An interesting manuscript of Sieyes, signed, undated, but seemingly prior to the Revolution, is reprinted by Dr. Cabanis (*Chronique Medicale*, pp. 90-94, 1 Feb., 1901). It is a very exact and sometimes revolting description of his state of health, and concludes as follows: "J'ai un faible tempérament. Le moindre effort, tout exercice un peu violent, excepté la promenade, me laissent une lassitude générale et des douleurs comme si j'avais été martelé. Je porte un visage très pâle, la peau sèche, se détachant en poussière par le frottement. Je suis très sensible au froid, malingre et très maigre. Cependant il me semble avoir le sentiment d'une certaine force, de quelque vigueur, mais ce n'est qu'un feu de paille." Throughout the Revolution, one finds references to his ill-health, but this "fire of straw" burned for eighty-eight years.

[15] Young, A., *Travels in France*, pp. 163-164; Baudot, *Notes His-*

Two of his qualities lend a touch of charm to the picture. He loved music, wrote down reflections concerning it from time to time, and had a collection of operatic pieces which he called " la catologue de ma petite musique ; " [16] and his letters to his father, which show real devotion to his sisters and a sincere regard for the health and welfare of his parents, are certain evidences of an affectionate nature.[17]

Traits more suited to the part he was to play also manifested themselves. First of all, his religious scepticism. His unhappiness at Saint Sulpice has already been mentioned. By the time that he had taken orders, that is, at the age of twenty-five, he had, as he expressed it, " freed himself from all superstitious sentiments and ideas," and his later correspondence, while revealing his father's deep piety, shows none at all on the part of the son.[8] Jesuits, Sulpicians, and mentors alike, however, agreed as to his intelligence, and the news of rapid intellectual progress must have gladdened the hearts of his parents. " The young man will do you honor," wrote Césarges in November, 1769, and his rise at Chartres bore out this prediction, at least in a worldly sense.[19]

toriques, p. 2 ; Brissot, *Mémoires*, vol. iii, p. 135, note ; *Notice de M. Fortoul*, quoted by Sainte-Beuve, *op. cit.*, vol. v, p. 191.

[16] *Ibid.*, vol. v, p. 192, Sainte-Beuve saw this collection ; *Notice*, pp. 14-15. The Swiss, Etienne Dumont, who met him in 1789, recorded that he loved music passionately and was thoroughly acquainted with its basic principles. Dumont, E., *Souvenirs sur Mirabeau*, p. 65.

[17] Teissier, *op. cit.*, pp. 136-139. " Mes deux soeurs sont, après vous et ma mère, ce que j'aime le mieux au monde " (letter, undated, but probably written in the winter of 1778). This and other like expressions bear all the evidences of spontaneous and unaffected feeling.

[18] *Notice*, pp. 15-16 ; letters published by Teissier, *op. cit.*, *passim*. The *Notice* (pp. 14-15, 16-18) informs us that through this part of his career he was careful never to preach or to confess, always seeking the rôle of an ecclesiastical administrator. At the same time he sweepingly condemns raising up children for an ecclesiastical career, concluding, " et ce crime se commetait au nom de la Divinité, comme si Dieu avoit besoin de service des hommes."

[19] *Ibid.*, pp. 10 ; 16-18 ; Sainte-Beuve, *op. cit.*, vol. v, pp. 191-192 ;

Even at this age, his mind worked powerfully and freely. He refused to follow any school of thought, the Encyclopedists, Condillac or Rousseau. He showed, then as always, a contempt for men's abilites, coupled with a desire to serve mankind by evolving a perfect political and social system, based upon the principle of harmonious unity. If Sieyes had been capable of passionate and all-compelling belief, this unity concept would have been a passion with him. He believed that all human knowledge could be brought into one sweet accord. " Lacking this," he wrote, " there are only independent minds, whose knowledge is good for nothing. Although they may store up much in their memories, they are really ignorant and have no use." To bring about the desired state of perfection, and to solve life's other problems, he proposed, simply and solely, the application of mental powers. " If thought were lost, adieu humanity." [20]

Another trait comes out strikingly in his correspondence. He was very ambitious of preferment, and failure to obtain it made him bitter. " I will give myself a livelihood or I will die," he wrote to his father in 1773,[21] and when, in 1778, Lubersac failed to get him a position at court, " that would take me to Versailles," he lashed out bitterly against his benefactor. " My bishop has tricked me; . . . he wants to make me his âme damnée at Tréguier. . . . I put no more faith in these men's promises than I do in the predictions of the almanac. But I pretend to because I cannot do any

Teissier, *op. cit.,* pp. 130, 133-4, especially the letters of Césarges to H. Sieyes, Nov., 1769, and Besplas to H. Sieyes, 26 April, 1774; Romilly, *op. cit.,* vol. i, pp. 77-78.

[20] Sainte-Beuve, *op. cit.,* vol. v, pp. 191; 200-208. The quotations are from extracts from Sieyes' early mss., cited by Sainte-Beuve. Sieyes belittled Buffon because the naturalist's conclusions were sometimes contradictory. This, Sieyes held, often made his generalisations only false unities.

[21] Teissier, *op. cit.,* E. J. Sieyes to H. Sieyes, 25 June, 1773.

better." [22]   So wrote the able sceptic, whose only use for the church was as a medium for his own advancement.

All through this period he read widely.   Bonnet, Condillac and Locke gave him the greatest satisfaction,[23] but his intellectual activity must have made him conversant with the other outstanding writers of his time.   Interesting possible connections appear between these authors specially mentioned by him and his own later ideas.   There is little enough in Bonnet's *Contemplation of Nature* to prove congenial, save for that naturalist philosopher's attempt to show that the world is primarily ordered and harmonious.[24]   But Condillac's rejection of the doctrine of innate ideas,[25] his support of the contract theory of government with his accompanying distinction between natural and positive law,[26] his hatred of inequality,[27] and his advocacy of representative government,[28] are all embodied in Sieyes' philosophy, and in his political teaching.

There are obvious points of similarity between Locke and

[22] *Ibid.*, p. 137, E. J. Sieyes to H. Sieyes, 3 April, 1778; pp. 138-9, same to same, for a continuation in this strain.

[23] *Notice*, p. 12.   These authors, and Adam Smith (mentioned directly in the *Observations—sur la nouvelle organisation de la France*, pp. 34-35) are the only ones of whom he ever speaks directly.

[24] Bonnet, Chas., *Contemplation de la Nature,* the whole work.   See also, Caraman, le Duc de, *Charles Bonnet*, pp. 204 *et seq.*

[25] Condillac, *Oeuvres*, vol. iii, pp. 3 *et seq.;* 121-122.   *Extrait raisonné du traité des sensations.*   And in English translation, *An Essay on the Origin of Human Knowledge,* the whole work.

[26] Condillac, *Oeuvres*, vol. iii, pp. 42-45; 506 *et seq.; cf.* Sieyes, *Qu'est-ce le tiers état,* pp. 65-68.   Both use the terms " droit naturel " and " droit positif " in exactly the same sense.

[27] Condillac, *Oeuvres*, vol. 21, pp. 403-404; vol. xvi, pp. 388-394.   His portrayal of the evils inherent in privilege is strikingly similar to that in Sieyes' *Essai sur les privilèges,* pp. 4, 15.

[28] Condillac, *Oeuvres,* vol. 21, pp. 377 *et seq.;* vol. ii, p. 383.   As will be noted later, the basis of Sieyes' whole political theory was representative government.

Sieyes. Both regarded private property as an inalienable and natural right; both turned to the people as the final political authority; both insisted upon representative government and majority rule; [29] and it is interesting to note that both lamented the inadequacies and imperfections of language as a vehicle of expression and suggested measures of reform.[30] These writers, and without doubt many others, helped to form the Abbé's manner of thinking during this early period. And it is easy to believe that Sieyes' natural dogmatism was intensified by his familiarity with the authoritative spirit which is characteristic of any long-established church.

In 1787 came an opportunity for Sieyes to take part in the political activities of the day. Necker's plan for establishing a new series of provincial assemblies (they were actually set up by him in two Generalities, Berry and Haute-Guyenne),[31] was adopted by Calonne and finally promulgated by a royal order of June, 1787, under the ministry of Lomenie de Brienne. These assemblies were to consist of three degrees, municipal, départemental and provincial. Each provincial assembly coincided in area with one of the old intendancies,[32] and was supposed to control the proceed-

[29] For Locke's views on these matters see Locke, J., *First Treatise on Government,* especially pp. 28-29, and 39 *et seq.* Also the *Second Treatise on Government,* ch. v, especially pp. 185 *et seq.;* ch. vii, pp. 231, 237; ch. viii, pp. 238-240; ch. x, pp. 266-7, 281; ch. xii, pp. 277 *et seq.;* ch. xiii, pp. 286-290; ch. xix, pp. 330-338.
For Sieyes' views on the sacredness of personal property see his Declaration of Rights in the *Procès-Verbaux de l'Assemblée Nationale,* vol. ii, arts. 6-7, 12 (20-21 Juillet, 1789). For the political ideas mentioned *vide infra,* ch. v, pp. 75 *et seq.,* and his constitutional plans of 1789, 1795, 1799.

[30] Locke, J., *An Essay Concerning Human Understanding,* vol. ii, pp. 6 *et seq.* and chs. 9, 10, 11. *Cf.* Sainte-Beuve, *Causeries de Lundi,* vol. v, pp. 196-199, for quotes from Sieyesian mss.

[31] Renouvin, P., *Les Assemblées provinciales de 1787,* pp. 46 *et seq.*

[32] *Ibid.,* pp. 100-101; 81-82; 87; Fromont, H., *Essai sur l'administration de l'assemblée provinciale de la généralité d'Orléans,* p. 598.

ings of the lesser gatherings within its sphere, regulate the distribution of taxes and advise as to abuses in their establishment and collection, and recommend to the ministry projects useful to the province. The king named half the members for the first meeting. They elected their colleagues and, while the three Estates were separately represented, the delegates all sat together.[33]

Sieyes was elected as a representative of the clergy to the provincial assembly of Orléans. This assembly, which included the area around Chartres, sat from 17 November to 22 December, its first and only session.[34] The President (the Duke of Luxembourg) appointed Sieyes a member of the Bureau of Public Welfare and of Agriculture, and a member of the Committee on the Twentieths.[35]

None of the papers emanating from the committees were signed, and there is nothing to show that Sieyes had any part in the lengthy reports of the Committee on Public Welfare and Agriculture, which were presented during December, 1787. But the report of the Committee on the Twentieths, with its terse, epigrammatic style and its keen denunciation of injury done to the common people, bears a striking resemblance, especially in certain paragraphs, to his later style as a pamphleteer.[36] This report asked the transformation of the

[33] Renouvin, *op. cit.*, pp. 104, 109.

[34] *Archives du Loiret*, C, 891. Tableau; C, 892, Procès-Verbal de l'Assemblée Provinciale.

[35] *Ibid.*, C, 892. Procès-Verbal. Session 19 Nov., 1787. The Twentieth was a government tax on incomes.

[36] *Ibid.*, session 30 Nov., 1787. Report of the Committee on the Twentieths. It is, of course, impossible to prove that Sieyes drew up this report, but the resemblance to his style, which so far as I know has been mentioned by no other writer, comes out in such paragraphs as the following :

" Quoi! tout homme pourroit abonner son fardeau, & une Province entière assemblée n'en auroit pas la compétence? D'ailleurs, si c'est un droit, on peut vous le communiquer; si c'est une prérogative, on peut

tax on incomes into a contract at a fixed rate, thus establishing certainty as to taxation and preventing arbitrary increase or dispensation. The Assembly adopted the project and humbly solicited its acceptance by the king. He granted their request but the plan aroused a storm of protest in the Generality and was never carried into effect.[37]

At the last session, 22 December, 1787, six members were elected to form an Intermediary Commission, which was to carry on the business of the Assembly until the next regular session. Sieyes was the one member of the clergy on this body. Lavoisier, who was a member of the Third Estate, was also chosen.[38] But the Abbé took no interest in its proceedings. He drew up, it is true, a plan of procedure, but it was not accepted.[39] The Procès-Verbal notes his absence from the first twenty-nine sessions, and a short interval of

vous l'accorder." And again — "L'abonnement, en effet, est une protection pour le malheureux en même temps qu'il est un frein pour le riche. Vous écarterez cette fréquente inquisition qui ne se repose jamais, tout ce système de vérifications qui ne s'arrêtent que devant les grands domaines et devant ceux à qui ils appartiennet. C'est votre justice et votre bienveillance qui s'adresseront à ceux qui croyaient être à l'abri de la loi parce qu'ils l'avaient éludée; c'est par vous qu'ils apprendront qu'il n'y a plus de dispenses et d'exceptions et que s'il en restait encore, vous ne les destineriez qu'à ceux en faveur desquels il n'y en à jamais eu."

It is also to be noted that Sieyes' two most zealous supporters, Lubersac and Césarges, were on this committee. Furthermore in 1789, Sieyes returned to the question of the vingtièmes—"Arrêté: que les vingtièmes sur les biens seront convertis en subvention, & que ce qui paroit n'être qu'un changement de nom facilitera pourtant l'égalisation de cet impôt." (*Délibérations à prendre*, p. 50.)

In view of these circumstances, we may safely ascribe to Sieyes a prominent part on the Committee, and it seems extremely probable that part, if not all, of the report was drawn up by him.

[37] *Archives du Loiret*, C. 892. *Procès-Verbal*, sessions of 30 Nov., 17, 21 Dec., 1787; Fromont, *op. cit.*, pp. 256 *et seq.*, 274.

[38] *Archives du Loiret*, C. 892, *Procès-Verbal*.

[39] Letter of Lavoisier, 16 March, 1788, quoted by Neton, *op. cit.*, pp. 584-585.

attendance was ended the last of May, 1788, when he went back to Paris.[40]

The provincial assemblies failed. Set among the crowding events of those last years before the deluge broke, they had neither the money nor the time necssary to work out their plans.[41] But Sieyes considered them very important. Writing early in 1789, he remarked that the single assembly of property owners, regardless of Orders, might well have led to the establishment of a community of interest, " and the nation would have ended where all nations ought to commence, in being one." [42] There can be no doubt that this experience strengthened his desire to amalgamate the Orders in the Estates General of 1789, and it is interesting, though possibly only a coincidence, that the départements of modern France, which owe their existence so largely to him, have approximately the same limits as the generalities represented by these provincial gatherings.[43]

Aside from his activities at Orléans, we have only glimpses of Sieyes during the years just before the Revolution. He must have been busy with his administrative duties at Chartres and Paris, but he found time for other matters as well. Brissot met him and Lubersac at Rotterdam, during the summer of 1787,[44] and it was in this same year that the abbé counselled the Parlement of Paris, just exiled to Troyes, to go immediately to the palace and force the arrest and hanging of the minister issuing such arbitrary orders. " The

---

[40] *Archives du Loiret,* C. 894, *Procès-Verbal de la Commission Intermédiaire.* Sieyes was also in the Départemental Assembly of Chartres and Dourdan, of which Lubersac was president, but there is nothing in the procès-verbal to distinguish his activities. (*Archives d'Eure et Loir,* C-1, C-2. These are at Chartres).

[41] Fromont, *op. cit.,* pp. 600-601.

[42] *Qu'est-ce le tiers état,* pp. 51-52.

[43] Fromont, *op. cit.,* pp. 583-586.

[44] Brissot de Warville, *Mémoires,* vol. ii, p. 436.

success of this measure was certain, but his advice did not prevail," he wrote later.[45]   So the leaven of revolt was working in him, fomented by the friends he made.   He became a Mason, joining the famous Lodge of the Nine Sisters, which counted Condorcet, Bailly, Pétion, Desmoulins, and Danton among its members,[46] and we may assume that about this time he began frequenting Madame Necker's famous salon, where Condorcet, Talleyrand and others, including the young Madame de Staël, foregathered.[47]

But the picture of him that one likes best is that given by Etienne Dumont, who says that the abbé spent a great part of his summers at Chartres, almost a recluse, reading little, but meditating much and doing a considerable amount of writing which he had not the patience to revise.[48]   He was preparing himself, consciously or unconsciously, for what was to come, and the advent was at hand.   Montesquieu, Rousseau, the Encyclopedists, had urged plans for reform, plans that appealed strongly to the middle classes and to the intelligentsia, and Paris, where Rousseau was read on the

[45] *Notice*, p. 20.

[46] Amiable, A., *Une Loge maçonnique d'avant 1789*, p. 4; Martin, G., *La Franc-maçonnerie française et la préparation de la révolution*, pp. 134-135.   See also a curious little book by Gassicourt, C., *Le Tombeau de Jacques Molai*, p. 63; and the citations from the papers of Cardinal de Bernis in connection with the Club of the Propaganda, given by Deschamps, N., *Les Sociétés secrètes et la société*, vol. ii, p. 138.

[47] Challamel, A., *Les Clubs contre-révolutionnaires*, p. 553.   In February, 1789, he was summoned to Montfort-l'Amaury as an elector for the clergy in the general assembly of the three estates, but took no part in the proceedings and was not elected. . . Thenard, " L'Abbé Sieyes électeur et élu, 1789," in *La Révolution française*, vol. xiv, pp. 1083-1089 (1888). For an interesting reference to this incident see the anonymous *Correspondance secrète inédite sur Louis XVI, Marie Antoinette, la cour et la ville, de 1777 à 1792*, vol. ii, p. 339.   Letters 12, 13: Paris, 22, 27 March, 1789.

[48] Dumont, E., *Souvenirs sur Mirabeau*, pp. 64-65.   Dumont had this information directly from Lubersac; cf. *Notice*, p. 20.

street corners, teemed with the spirit of change.[49]   Religion, which might have been a stabilizing influence, had largely lost its hold upon the upper classes, and even to a considerable extent upon the peasantry.[50]   And the steadily increasing financial confusion, which a succession of Louis XVI's ministers had been unable to clarify, acted upon the government like the weight of a heavy hand constantly pushing in the direction of concession and change.   A strange and fateful concatenation of events!   It was bound to produce new leaders, and among these Sieyes was to take a place in the front rank.

[49] For the latest summary of the philosophers' plans and influence see Gottschalk, L. R., *The Era of the French Revolution,* pp. 57-84.

[50] Aulard, A., *Christianity and the French Revolution,* pp. 31 *et seq.*

CHAPTER II

THE PAMPHLETEER

ON 5 July, 1788, King Louis XVI issued an Order in Council asking everyone in France who knew or could find out anything about the Estates General (their last meeting had been in 1614) to communicate their information to the Keeper of the Seals. One month later a royal order fixed 1 May, 1789, as the day on which the Estates should formally convene.[1]

Such a momentous event inevitably called forth quantities of tracts and pamphlets from the politically minded, and some of the men who wrote, such as Marat, Target and Mounier, were destined to become famous in the Revolution.[2] But none of these contributions received more notice or more applause than the terse and epigrammatic writings of a certain member of the upper clergy.

In the summer of 1788, while Sieyes was enjoying the pleasures of country life not far from Paris, he composed his first pamphlet, the *Views on the Means of Execution of which the French Representatives can avail themselves in 1789.* But on his return to the capital, alarmed by the possibility that the nobles would have a predominant place in the coming Assembly, he suspended its publication while he wrote and had distributed two others, the *Essay on Privileges,* and *What is the Third Estate.* These three tracts

[1] Brette, A., *Recueil de documents relatifs à la convocation des États Généraux de 1789,* vol. i, pp. 19-23.

[2] For information in regard to these pamphlets, see the articles by Garrett, M. B., "A Critical Bibliography of the Pamphlet Literature Published in France between 5 July and 27 December, 1788," and "The Pamphlet Crisis in France in 1789," in the *Howard College Bulletin,* April, 1925 and June, 1927.

were soon followed by a fourth, the *Plan of Deliberations,*[3] after which he wrote no more prior to the institution of the National Assembly.

The *Essay on Privileges* was published in November, 1788, as a terrific indictment of political and social inequality. Beginning with the dogmatic assertion that liberty is anterior to society, and that the origin of all law lies in the great natural law that men shall not do harm to one another, Sieyes argues that in a truly social state men are essentially equal. All privileges, then, save honorary ones accorded by the people as special rewards, are vicious in character. They are opposed to the supreme ends of all political society, which are the maintenance of the widest individual liberty, and the perpetuation of equality.[4] Such is the keynote of this whole bitter attack. In moving terms he depicts the effects of such a system: the creation of a class that thinks of itself rather than of the nation's interests, and regards the people as debased and born to serve; the inflation of pride and vanity; the exaltation of intrigue; the degradation of honest work, which the so-called upper classes consider beneath them.[5] Privilege is an evil more dangerous than any other, for " it is more intimately connected with the social organisation; it corrupts more profoundly; more interests devote themselves to defending it. Here, certainly, are motives for rousing the zeal of true patriots." [6] Every page is vibrant with his

[3] A copy of the *Délibérations* in the White library at Cornell attributes (p. 7, footnote) its authorship to Cerutti, but its style would mark it as the work of Sieyes. He claims it explicitly (*Notice*, pp. 25-26), and all authorities attribute it to him (see, among others, Bloch, *op. cit.*, vol. i, pp. xii-xiii, and Buchez et Roux, *op. cit.*, vol. i, pp. 284-285).

[4] *Essai sur les privilèges*, pp. 2-4, 16-17.

[5] *Ibid.*, pp. 9, 10-11, 15, 18 *et. seq.*, 25-26. He repeatedly stresses his contention that the great body of non-privileged, the masses of the people, are the real French nation (pp. 4-5, 9, 11, note 2).

[6] *Ibid.*, p. 24.

conviction that the people are laboring under a great injustice. Clear, concise, direct, it expressed the discontent of the bourgeoisie, and more significantly, perhaps, that envious dislike of all superiority which is characteristic of humanity.

Early in January, 1789,[7] appeared the most influential pamphlet, *What is the Third Estate*. The three questions at the beginning give its underlying theme. " What is the Third Estate? Everything. What has it been heretofore in the political order? Nothing. What does it ask? To become something." [8] Then comes a series of arguments, very skillfully constructed to show that the Third Estate, ninety-five per cent of the population, sustains society; that it has " within itself all that is necessary to form a complete nation; " and that the nobility, a stranger in the midst because of its special interests and prerogatives, forms an *imperium in imperio* which is unauthorized by the people and is inimical to the welfare of the nation.[9]

The Third Estate, he continues, has a right to complain. It is enslaved, because freedom is only possible through rights equally and completely shared, and the nation itself cannot become free when the Third Estate is not free. In fact, the nation, of which the Third Estate is the central part and portion, cannot be said to exist unless it has a common law and a common representation. Furthermore, in past meetings of the Estates, the Third has been too often represented by newly created nobles and privileged char-

[7] Garret, M. B., " A Critical Bibliography, etc.," in the *Howard College Bulletin* (April, 1925), pp. 24-25.

[8] *Qu'est-ce que le tiers état*, p. 27. He prefaced it with a note that reserves to the philosopher the right of contemplating perfection, admitting that the executive must set his sails to suit the wind.

[9] *Ibid.*, pp. 28-33. Mention has already been made of Sieyes' early passion for an harmonious and unitary social order (*vide supra*, ch. i, p. 16. These pamphlets show the persistence of this idea and his application of it to the political situation in 1789.

acters. Thus its interests have not received proper attention and its political rights have been rendered null.[10] These grievances must be remedied in the coming assembly. Justice and equality must be obtained. The representatives of the masses must be chosen from their own ranks; they must equal in number those of the other two orders; voting must be by head and not by order. He argues these points at length against possible objections.[11]

In the fifth chapter he outlines a set of political principles for the guidance of the nation, and in so doing states his theory of government which is that of Rousseau's *Social Contract,* plus a representative system.[12] Individuals voluntarily unite to form a community. Thus the nation is brought into existence. They agree to act in common, and so is first manifested the " general will " which is the basis of the organisation. Increase of numbers necessitates the institution of representative government. But this government is limited in its powers. Its will is only a " representative general will " and is subject to control by the will of the nation (volonté national),[13] which is always the source

[10] *Ibid.,* pp. 32-36.

[11] *Ibid.,* pp. 37-50. Representation equal in numbers to that of the other two orders had been granted by the time this pamphlet appeared (Brette, A., *op. cit.,* vol. i, p. 37. Royal order of 27 December, 1788).

[12] I am certain that he does not mention Rousseau in any of his writings now extant. Sieyes had no love for appealing to authorities other than himself. But Sainte-Beuve (*op. cit.,* vol. v, pp. 194-195) quotes MSS. notes which show that Sieyes, while accepting Rousseau's views on the origin of society, denies him any part in establishing the " principles of the social art " (" principes de l'art social ") of which the abbé considered himself the great elucidator. The fact remains, however, that this chapter, with its insistence upon the supremacy of the nation and the national will, reproduces Rousseau's chief arguments as to sovereignty. (*Cf. Contrat Social,* bk. iv, chs. 1-4). Sieyes uses the term " contrat social " (*Qu'est-ce que le tiers état,* p. 54).

[13] *Ibid.,* pp. 64-75. The decision of the majority represents the national will, and expresses itself in constitutional laws untouchable by governing

of the law and the government. The nation is the supreme entity. It exists before all and is the origin of all. Its will is always legal, in fact it is the law itself. The nation alone cannot be bound, and it alone, by means of a special representative assembly vested with extraordinary powers, can determine or change the constitution. Such an assembly should be called so that France may obtain the blessings of constitutional government.[14]

As to immediate steps, he suggests that the Third might assemble alone. It represents twenty-five million people, and if it cannot form the Estates General it will constitute a National Assembly. Or it might assemble and refuse to act, thus forcing a special election to a constitutional convention.[15] He closes with a final attack upon privilege.[16] The whole pamphlet is an exaltation of political equality, and a very able, closely knit argument for a representative government deriving its authority from the consent of the governed.

The *Views on the Means of Execution,* which came out a few weeks later, repeats what he had already published, be-

bodies (*ibid.,* pp. 66-67, 73-75). For the expression "representative general will" I am indebted to Dunning, W. A., *A History of Political Theory from Rousseau to Spencer,* p. 103.

[14] *Ibid.,* pp. 64, 69-71, 76. As events proved, Sieyes was very willing to waive this last point.

[15] *Ibid.,* pp. 79-81, 70-71, 83. Throughout the latter part of this pamphlet he repeatedly refers to a future "National Assembly." He urges unity in very marked fashion. To him, the Third Estate, whose representatives are alone the custodians of the national will, is the only feasible center for unity in France (p. 82).

[16] *Ibid.,* pp. 88-93. En attendant, il est impossible de dire quelle place deux corps privilégiés doivent occuper dans l'ordre social; c'est demander quelle place l'on veut assigner, dans le corps d'un malade, à l'humeur maligne qui le mine et le tourmente. Il faut la *neutraliser,* il faut rétablir la santé et le jeu de tous les organes assez bien pour qu'il ne s'y forme plus de ces combinaisons morbifiques, capables de vicier les principes les plus essentiels de la vitalité (p. 93). The figure easily might have been suggested by his own frail health.

sides giving special attention to the financial situation. It begins by asserting that France, a nation that is only now awakening from sloth and slumber, needs a constitution based on reason and principles rather than upon outworn historical precedents. Then follows a lengthy argument as to the right of the nation to make its own laws by means of a duly constituted representative assembly. A nation endowed with such a prerogative should, of course, have final authority in fiscal matters, and the pamphlet turns to a consideration of bankruptcy as a remedy for the government's financial ills.[17]

Starting from the premise that national bankruptcy is a crime because it negates the sacredness of personal property, he argues that, as the nation would have no right to declare itself bankrupt, no such right is vested in the king. Obviously fearful of such executive action, he urges that the Estates General should immediately assume control of the treasury and consolidate the debt, after which they could use the straits to which the government had been reduced as a lever in obtaining a good constitution, " the sole basis of order, welfare and reform." This constitution should provide for the separation of the legislative, executive and judicial departments, and be a nucleus around which educational, fiscal and other reforms could be grouped.[18] The " National Assembly," the medium for expression of the general will, must be a permanent body, and have full liberty of speech and action.[19]

[17] *Vues sur les moyens*, pp. 1-3, 10 *et seq.*, 53 *et seq.* In this work, especially pp. 14-23, one finds again the " general will " idea of Rousseau. Sieyes' belief in his own ability to furnish the reason and principles necessary for a good constitution is amusingly plain. See especially pp. 1-3.

[18] *Ibid.*, pp. 102, 112, 118, 121-123, 135 *et seq.* A new system of taxation is strongly urged (pp. 103-104).

[19] *Ibid.*, pp. 75, 127-128, 130.

The chief direct attack is upon the ministry, which is flayed for not having taken competent financial measures. No project for a special constitutional convention appears, and there is no great outcry against the Estates General sitting by Orders. Fiscal problems take precedence over all others, but the underlying theme is the right of the nation to control, through its representatives, its own affairs.

The *Plan of Deliberations,* drawn up as advice to local deputies, but so constructed as to contain many suggestions for the National Assembly, divides itself into three parts. First, the needs of each local assembly. Here mention is made of the necessary political framework, but emphasis is laid upon fair and full representation of that vital part of the nation, the Third Estate. The privileged classes are unmercifully castigated, and criticism is levelled at indirect elections and plural voting, and at the custom of the Third's electing its representatives from the other two Orders.[20] Secondly, there is a discussion of the public needs, wherein is urged specific limitation of the power of the executive; a permanent National Assembly, deliberating freely and fully; a declaration of rights and a constitution; territorial redivision of France; thorough financial reforms by the legislature, which shall control the nation's pursestrings.[21] Lastly, advice is given concerning the election of deputies and their powers, this being a reiterated warning against local, imperative mandates, and an assertion that the deputies represent, not localities, but the nation as a whole. He closes with a paean of praise to representative government, and the assertion that " to the deputies of 1789 is confided the fate of France." [22]   On the whole, it contains many of the charges

---

[20] *Instruction donnée par S. A. S. Monseigneur le duc d'Orléans à ses représentants aux bailliages. Suivie de délibérations à prendre dans les assemblées,* pp. 1-21.

[21] *Délibérations,* pp. 22-60.

[22] *Ibid.,* pp. 60-67.

and complaints that he had already made, together with his most cherished constructive suggestions.

These four pamphlets contain the Sieyesian program, and are, in fact, an excellent outline of the whole reform movement that was so rapidly gathering headway. The demand for a declaration of rights and for a constitution; the onslaught upon privilege; the recognition of the people as the one basis upon which to erect a system of representative government; the separation of the executive from the legislative with the latter holding the pursestrings . . . all these are brought forward with epigrammatic force and clearness. The Revolution, it might seem, had found a leader.

What was the effect of these pamphlets, and how did they redound to the credit or discredit of Sieyes?

The complaints they register, the chief demands which they embody, were certainly neither new nor original. It is easy enough to find tract after tract attacking privilege, urging economic reform, insisting upon the overwhelming importance of the Third and its right to at least one-half the representation in the Estates General.[23] Two of the most influential pamphlets of this whole period came out before the writings of Sieyes. The Comte d'Antraigues' *Memoir Concerning the Estates General* appeared in 1788 and went

[23] Such as, for instance, Berenger, L. P., *Les Quatre états de la France* (Paris, 1789), pp. 8, 18-19; Anon., *Projet d'alliance matrimoniale entre M. Tiers-État et Madame Noblesse* (Paris, s. d.), pp. 3-4; Anon., *Le Triomphe du tiers-état* (Paris, 1789), pp. 5-6, 14 et seq.; Montesquieu-Fezenac, Marq. A. P. de, *Aux trois ordres de la nation* (Paris, s. d), pp. 7, 12-14, 21-24. And "glorias," "magnificats" and "holy weeks" without number, none of which show any direct evidence of Sieyes' influence. The political liberals in France had, during 1787-1788, formed a group that was known as the Nationals. This demanded immediate calling of the Estates General, and had a program asking for a constitution, the abolition of privileges, restoration of financial order and the repudiation of bankruptcy as a national remedy. Carré, H., in Lavisse, E., *Histoire de France*, vol. ix, pp. 356, 366-367.

through at least two editions in that year.[24]   This work attacks privilege; asserts that the Third Estate is the people; that the people are the basis of the state, are, in fact, the state itself; that the Third's deputies should equal those of the other two Orders; and that the Estates General should control taxation.[25]   These arguments were the chief stock in trade of Sieyes.   Cerutti was the author of a tract,[26] which asserted the predominance of the Third, and argued for equality of representation.   Sieyes cited this pamphlet several times in his own writing.[27]

The abbé's proposals for putting the Third in immediate possession of its rights, such as general elections without distinction as to Order, were none of them followed,[28] and Champion has conclusively demonstrated that the *Plan of Deliberations,* with its lack of emphasis upon local grievances,

[24] Mirabeau, "Huitième lettre à ses commettans," in the *Courrier de Provence,* vol. i, 30 May–4 June, 1789.   For the great influence of this pamphlet, see Champion, E., "La Conversion du Comte d'Antraigues," in *La Révolution française,* vol. xxv, 1894, p. 6, note 2, and pp. 6–7.

[25] Antraigues, Cte. d'., *Mémoire sur les états-généraux,* pp. 20, 100 *et seq.,* 160, 171, 246–247, 257.   He asserts (p. 246): "le tiers état est le peuple, & le peuple est la base de l'état; il est l'état lui-même. . . . c'est dans le peuple que réside la toute-puissance nationale; c'est par lui que tout l'état existe, & pour lui seul qu'il doit exister."   Sieyes uses very similar language.   In *Qu'est-ce que le tiers etat* (pp. 66–67), he says: "La nation existe avant tout, elle est l'origine de tout.   Sa volonté est toujours légale, elle est la loi elle-même.   Avant elle et au-dessus d'elle il n'y a que le droit naturel . . . La nation est tout ce qu'elle peut être par cela seul qu'elle est."

[26] *Mémoire pour le peuple français.*   There is a reprint in *La Révolution française* (vol. xv, 1888), with an introduction by F. A. Aulard entitled "Un Pamphlet de Cerutti."   There were two editions of this pamphlet in 1788.

[27] *Cf.* the Cerutti pamphlet, p. 60, and *Qu'est-ce que le tiers état,* p. 52.   See also Aulard's comment, "Un pamphlet de Cerutti," in *La Révolution française,* vol. xv, p. 55.

[28] *Qu'est-ce que le tiers état,* chap. vi, pp. 79 *et seq.*   See Champion's comment—Introduction, p. iii.

could have had little influence in the rural communities to which it was distributed.[29]

But despite these mitigating circumstances, Sieyes was a distinct and powerful force during this period. Everyone of his pamphlets was reprinted,[30] and a host of contemporaries bear witness to their influence.[31] *What is the Third Estate* eclipsed the others. " It perverted the public," said Malouet,[32] and many other memoir writers, friends and foes alike, recognized its powerful effect.[33] It was mentioned

[29] Champion, E., *La France d'après les cahiers de 1789*, p. 24, note 1; p. 95, note 1. The lawyers who drew up many of the cahiers may have been influenced. See Bloch, C. (ed.), *Cahiers de doléances du bailliage d'Orléans*, vol. i, p. xi, note 1.

[30] I have found, for the year 1789, two editions of the *Essay on Privileges*, two of the *Views*, four of the *Plan of Deliberations* and four of *What is the Third Estate*.

[31] Dumont, E., *Souvenirs*, pp. 65-66; Barras, P. F. J. N., *Mémoires*, vol. ii, p. 378; Oelsner, K. E., *Des Opinions politiques du citoyen Sieyes*, p. 267; *Moniteur*, 20 Nov., 1789—review of Saint-Pierre's *Voeux d'un solitaire*; *ibid.*, 2 Jan., 1790—Revolutionary books and pamphlets banned by the Spanish Holy Office. Editorial comment; *ibid.*, 30 thermidor, VII. Garat, speaking in the Ancients, séance 29 thermidor, VII (16 Aug., 1799). See also (reprinted in Sainte-Beuve, *op. cit.*, vol. v, p. 206), Mirabeau's letter to Sieyes (23 Feb., 1789), thanking him for the pamphlets on privilege and the third estate—" Il y a donc un homme en France." . . . et certes un homme appelé à nous guide dans l'assemblée nationale qui va décréter notre destinée." The Abbé Brun de la Combe, in an attack upon ultra-liberal opinion in 1789, singled out Sieyes as one most capable of deceiving the people . . . " Il suffit d'abattre le fantome élevé par les illusions les plus susceptibles d'éblouir. Dans cette vue, nous avons cru devoir nous borner à l'examen des principes de M. l'Abbé Syeyes, comme à ceux d'un Ecrivain distingué, dont les ouvrages se trouvent entre les mains de tout le monde."—*Doutes sur les principes de M. l'Abbé Syeyes concernant la constitution nationale*, p. 4.

[32] *Mémoires*, vol. i, p. 266; Report had it that it sold 30,000 copies in three weeks. (*Ibid.*, ii, p. 217, note 3). Baudot, who disliked Sieyes, said that it " lui avait crée une foule d'enthousiastes."—Baudot, M. A., *Notes historiques sur la convention nationale, le directoire, l'empire et l'exil des votants*, p. 225.

[33] Oelsner, K. E., *op. cit.*, pp. 90191. It did much, he says, " à répandre

time and again by contemporaries as evidence of the abbé's greatness, and it must have bulked large in the surreptitious shipments of his writings into Spain.[34]

Furthermore, other pamphleteers were influenced. Marat, in his celebrated *Offering to the Country*, uses arguments strikingly similar in tenor and sometimes in language to those of Sieyes;[35] and Camille Desmoulins, in a pamphlet called *Free France*, openly praises Sieyes as one of the defenders of the people, entitles one of his own chapters " Qu' est-ce qu' une constitution " and uses the abbé's arguments and language.[36]

dans toutes les âmes le feu de patriotisme jusqu'alors inconnu; " Barère, B., *Mémoires*, vol. iv, p. 427.—" La fortune de cet ouvrage vient de l'esprit de nationalité qui l'avait inspiré, dans une époque où il n'y avait pas encore de nation en France . . . ; " Brissot, *op. cit.*, vol. iii, p. 135; Barras, *op. cit.*, vol. ii, p. 378; Students of the period add their testimony: Monin, H., *L'état de Paris en 1789*, p. 246, and Chassin, Ch.-L., *Les Élections et les cahiers de Paris en 1789*, vol. i, p. 174, and vol. iv, pp. 24-25.

[34] For statements in regard to contemporary enthusiasm, based on documentary evidence, see *ibid.*, vol. ii, pp. 309-312; and vol. iii, p. 251; and Challamel, A., *Les Clubs contre-révolutionnaires*, p. 425. In January of 1791, there appeared in the *Révolutions de Paris* (vol. vii, no. 81, 22-29 Jan., 1791), a curious editorial entitled " Qu'est-ce le peûple? " It exalts the rôle of the people, in a manner obviously copied after Sieyes' pamphlet. For the shipment of his pamphlets into Spain, see Mousset, A., *Un Témoin ignoré de la révolution. Le comte de Fernan Nûnez, ambassadeur d'Espagne à Paris*, p. 161, annexe 2 à la lettre (de Nûnez) à Floridablanca, 9 octobre, 1790.

[35] Marat, *Offrande à la patrie* (Paris, 1789). Compare especially pp. 1-4, 6, 10-11, 36, to *Qu'est-ce que le tiers ètat*, pp. 67-69. Both assert the right of the nation to authority and power; both call upon the Third, which has been nothing but has a right to be everything; and both place their hopes for the future in the national assembly.

[36] *La France libre*, pp. 4-8, 9 et seq.; on pp. 14-15, Camille expresses himself in the following fashion: " Il est donc incontestable que les députés des communes de France représentant la presque universalité de la nation, leur volonté est la volonté générale; c'est la loi elle-même." In *Qu'est-ce que le tiers état*, p. 67, Sieyes, in stressing the authority of the nation, says: " La nation existe avant tout, elle est l'origine de tout. Sa volonté est toujours légale, elle est la loi elle-même." Now, important as

The result of this rise to prominence [37] was manifested on 19 May. On that day, the assembly of the Parisian Third Estate, after a lengthy discussion, elected Sieyes as their last (twentieth) delegate to the Estates General. There was some difficulty, for the assembly had passed a resolution formally excluding from candidacy all nobles and ecclesiastics.[38] But Bailly's failure to record in the minutes the prohibition of the clergy, made its evasion possible, and, as he said, " a large part of the electors felt that Sieyes' merit was worthy of high consideration. He had been exceedingly useful to the state, and especially to the Third, whose cause he had sustained." [39]

The protest against him was carried to the Estates General but it did not avail. On 14 June, the Third formally ratified his admittance as one of the deputies of the commons.[40] The opportunity for translating his theories into practice was at hand.

Sieyes considered the representatives of the nation, he only gave complete and final authority to the nation itself. (*Ibid.*, pp. 66-67.) Camille twisted his argument about, or perhaps one should say that he carried it a step further, and gave final authority to the representatives of the general will.

[37] Besides his pamphleteering, Sieyes was also one of the founders of the Club de Valois, a sort of debating society which was under the wing of the Duc d'Orléans and was established 11 February, 1789. Lafayette, Talleyrand, Condorcet, the Lameths, also belonged to this club.—Challamel, *op. cit.*, pp. 31-35.

[38] Sieyes himself had suggested that exclusion.—*Délibérations à prendre*, p. 19.

[39] Chassin, *op. cit.*, vol. iii, pp. 250-251. He was elected on the third ballot. Eight electors signed a protest on account of his being an ecclesiastic; Robiquet, P., *Le Personnel municipal de Paris pendant la révolution*, p. 13; Bailly, J. S., *Mémoires*, vol. i, pp. 75-79.

[40] Chassin, *op. cit.*, vol. iii, p. 251; *Procès-Verbal de l'Assemblée des Communes et de l'Assemblée Nationale* (Paris et Versailles), vol. i, p. 70; the king received him, and the other deputies not yet presented, on 24 May.—Letter of De Brezé to the President of the Third.— *Point du Jour.*, vol. i, part i, p. 132).

CHAPTER III

HIS PLACE IN THE REVOLUTION.[1] CONSTITUENT TO CONVENTION

THROUGHOUT May and the first part of June, 1789, the assembly of the Third sat alone. Equal in numbers to the other two groups, it could find no means of forcing them to coalesce with it in a verification of credentials, the first step toward a unified body of delegates representing France as a whole. Repeated consultations between the Orders had been useless[2] and the Third was becoming vexed and weary.[3] On 10 June, the commissioners of the Third announced that the conciliation conferences were at an end, the nobles remaining refractory. Immediately Sieyes rose. Asserting that the time for action had come, he moved that the other Orders be given a final summons and told that if they did not come over immediately, verification would proceed without them.[4]

---

[1] I propose to show in this and the following chapter the part played by Sieyes from 1789 to 1799, emphasizing only his significant rôles.

[2] *Le Point du jour*, vol. i, pt. i, pp. 124 *et seq.*, 137 *et seq.*, 299 *et seq.* Mirabeau could scarcely be called a supporter of radical measures at this time, although he did seek the unification of the Orders. . . *Ibid.*, pp. 117 *et seq.*, 164 *et seq.*, 297 *et seq.* In treating the events of these June days I have used the *Procès-Verbal de l'assemblée des communes et de l'assemblée nationale*, for checking and verification.

[3] See the reception of Malouet's proposal for separate verification of powers. . . *Point du jour*, vol. i, pt. i, pp. 327-329.

[4] *Ibid.*, vol. i, pt. i, pp. 339-341; *Moniteur*, 10 June, 1789; *Journal des Etats Généraux convoqués par Louis XVI* (Paris, 1789), vol. i, pp.

There were some feeble objections but no important opposition, Target and Mirabeau both supported the motion, and it passed by a large plurality. The privileged Orders took it under consideration and the Third proceeded at once to the verification of powers according to a plan proposed by the abbé. So the first step in the Revolution was made, with Sieyes as the leader.[5]

The Third now began to show evidence of a bolder and more decided spirit, especially as the curés were drifting over to their ranks.[6] By 15 June, verification had been completed and on that day Sieyes took the lead. He moved that, inasmuch as this assembly represented at least ninety-six per cent of the nation, " It must be concluded that it, and it alone, can interpret the general will of the nation;[7] . . . it is the judge-

53-56. According to the *Journal* and the *Moniteur,* they must come within an hour, but the *Point du jour's* report gives them a day.

The phrasing of this motion shows that Sieyes was proceeding along the lines of political theory laid down in his writings. The Third, representing the majority of the French people, was the real representative of the nation. The others (deputies of the clergy and nobility) were, in his eyes, only recalcitrants who could be disregarded, if necessary, in going about the nation's business. It was the application of his convictions as to representative government and majority rule (*vide infra*, chap. v).

[5] *Journal des Etats Généraux,* vol. i, états, p. 57; *Point du Jour,* vol. i, pt. i, pp. 344, 349, 353-354, sessions of 11-13 June, 1789; Bailly, *Mémoires,* vol. i, pp. 165, 176. In regard to this event, Bailly remarks: . . . je suis porté à croire qu'il était le seul qui, dans ces circonstances nouvelles, pût avoir une idée assez nette des pouvoirs pour tracer cette marche de la sommation de l'appel du défaut, et qui dans la suite, par une conséquence de ses principes, pût indiquer un mode de constitution, qui nous laissait nos droits, sans détruire ceux des autres ordres, et qui, en nous plaçant au centre d'activité, nous établissait seuls agissans en les laissant en demeure et dans leur tort.

[6] *Point du Jour,* vol. i, pp. 346-357; *Journal des Etats Généraux,* vol. i, états, pp. 63, 66, 72-77, 83-84, 87. See especially the speeches of Barnave and Robespierre. Gregoire was one of the five curés who came over on the fifteenth.

[7] Majority rule and representative government, beginning to take concrete form.

ment, then, of this assembly that the common work of national restoration can and ought immediately to be commenced by the deputies here present . . .," and he ended by proposing that they adopt the title of " assembly of the recognized and verified representatives of the French nation." [8] The substance of this motion received practically unanimous consent, but others proposed different titles. After two days' debate, Sieyes shifted his ground, accepting the designation proposed by another deputy, Le Grand . . . " The National Assembly." [9] Thus amended, Sieyes' motion passed by a majority of over 400.[10]

Another very significant step had been taken under the abbé's leadership, and on the seventeenth, " When Sieyes entered the hall, the entire assembly, seized by a feeling of respect, rose spontaneously to receive him, and applause resounded from all sides." [11]

Naturally, enough, active participation in the affairs of the Assembly followed. He was at the Tennis Court on 20 June, where he signed the oath that the deputies would never separate until they had given France a constitution, and he

[8] *Journal des Etats Généraux,* vol. i, états, pp. 89-90. The motions of Mirabeau and Mounier were in practical agreement with that of Sieyes, save as to the title of the assembly.

[9] Le Grand, an obscure deputy, proposed this title on June 16. . . (*Point du Jour,* vol. i, pt. i, p. 395). But the term was not new. Lafayette had suggested the summoning of a " National Assembly " in 1787 (*Mémoires,* vol. ii, p. 177). The Royal Order of 5 July, 1788, referred to a " truly national assembly " (Brette, *op. cit.,* vol. i, p. 20). Sieyes himself had used the term repeatedly in his most famous pamphlet (*Qu'est-ce que le tiers état,* pp. 79, 81, 83-84, 88), and Mirabeau also used it several times in his speeches on 5, 8, and 15 June (*Point du Jour.,* vol. i, pt. i, pp. 282-283, 330, 372). The idea of having an assembly that represented the nation was widespread. Nevertheless, the assumption of the title was a bold step. Dumont believed that it was Sieyes' intention from the first (*Souvenirs,* p. 74).

[10] *Point du Jour.,* vol. i, pt. 2, p. 5.

[11] Dumont, *Souvenirs,* pp. 80-81.

was among those counselling immediate removal of the Assembly to Paris,[12] advice which did not prevail. On the famous day of 23 June, when the king commanded the deputies to separate immediately and meet thereafter only by Orders, he supported the rebellious Assembly in its refusal to obey, saying: " Gentlemen, you are today, what you were yesterday." It was probably a day or so later that he made a motion which was carried, decreeing the persons of the deputies inviolable and the meetings of the Assembly free and public.[13]

So far, the abbé had made a record of which he, as a liberal, might well be proud. He had led in changing the Estates General into a National Assembly (for the nobles soon joined the clergy in coming over), and, the weak efforts of the king to annul this action proving fruitless, the Assembly was thereafter to legislate as representative of the national will. It was a great change, for good or ill, and Sieyes had been the foremost leader in effecting it.

The summer and fall of 1789 were to witness further strenuous exertions upon his part. It was quite in the order of things that he should be made a member of the Committee on Rules, and be elected one of the six secretaries of the Assembly. After the fall of the Bastille, he was prominent among the members sent to Paris to help in restoring order, and when, on 14 July, the Committee on the Constitution was chosen, he was among the eight deputies elected. For about

[12] Mallet du Pan, *Mercure Britannique,* vol. v, p. 19, 25 Jan., 1800; Mallet du Pan, *Memoirs and Correspondance,* vol. i, p. 169. See also Aulard's account of the Tennis Court Oath (*La Révolution française,* vol. xvii, p. 15, 1889).

[13] The best analysis of the sources in regard to this famous session is made by Brette, A., " La Séance royale du 23 Juin, 1789 " in *La Révolution française,* vol. 23, pp. 55-62, 1892). For a report of Sieyes' further advice along this line, in the session of 8 July, see the *Courrier de Provence,* vol. i, p. 17, Mirabeau's eighteenth letter to his constituents.

three months the abbé was one of the leaders on this committee.[14]

All through this period he was the staunch exponent of the program that he had foreshadowed in his writings. From the first he had been an advocate of a declaration of rights,[15] and in July he drew up a model that was widely read and very popular.[16]   During July and August, various drafts were discussed in the Committee of the Constitution and that of Sieyes was among the most favored, only being superseded by that of the sixth bureau of the assembly.[17]   The final declaration shows no distinctive mark of his influence, for the projects of Mounier, Target and Lafayette contain between them all of Sieyes' proposals, but certainly his ideas lent weight to the whole project.   He was a leading exponent of the political division into " active " and " passive " citizens which was adopted by the constitution-makers,[18] and, above

[14] *Procès-Verbal*, vol. i, 19 June, 1789, p. 5; 3 July, 1789, p. 10; 14 July, p. 5; 16 July, pp. 2-3; Robiquet, P., *Le Personnel municipal de Paris pendant la révolution*, pp. 28-29. Mounier and Talleyrand were among the members of the Committee on the Constitution. The records of the Committee, such as they are, may be found in the Archives Nationales scattered throughout series C and in D-IV. They give no information of value as to the parts played by the individual members. No procès-verbal exists. But Sieyes' activity on the committee cannot be doubted, as is shown in the succeeding pages. Of course there is always the more or less questionable evidence of the memoir writers. For reference to his being an important figure on the Committee, see Baudot, M.A., *Notes Historiques*, p. 220, and Brissot, *Mémoires*, vol. ii, pp. 256-257; vol. iii, pp. 134-136.

[15] *Délibérations à prendre*, p. 31.

[16] *Préliminaire de la constitution; reconnaissance et exposition raisonnée des droits de l'homme et du citoyen.* There were eight editions of it, varying somewhat as to form and title, but of the same general content and program.

[17] Mounier, *Exposé de la conduite de M. Mounier*, p. 23. *Point du Jour.*, vol. ii, p. 163, session of 19 Aug., 1789; *Procès-Verbal*, vol. ii, 27 July, 1789, p. 6, and vol. iii, 19 Aug., 1789, p. 8.

[18] *Quelques idées de constitution applicables à la ville de Paris en*

all, his was the guiding hand in the establishment of a representative system and the reorganisation of France into départements.

In the *Deliberations,* and in a pamphlet written for the Parisian electors, he had outlined a plan of national representation and had demanded new territorial divisions.[19] On 7 September he brought this project to the attention of the Assembly, but that body was busily engaged in debating the single chamber and the suspensive veto, matters which were

juillet, 1789, p. 21; *Procès-Verbal,* vol. ii, " Préliminaire de la constitution," pp. 18-23. This distinction was first officially sanctioned by the Committee on the Constitution in its report of 29 Sept., 1789 (*Procès-Verval,* vol. v, pt. i, p. 8). As to ʻSieyes' connection with it, Aulard says: " It was he who first used the terms 'active' and 'passive' and outlined those formulae from which sprang the whole bourgeoise organisation" (*Histoire politique de la révolution française,* pp. 61-62). But it is well to note that Sieyes bears little or no responsibility for the real franchise limitations that sprang from this plan. His original idea (*Quelques idées de constitution,* pp. 19-22) had been a voluntary tax of three livres for participation in the primary assemblies, and twelve livres for eligibility as a representative. Thouret's report for the Committee of the Constitution (*Archives Parlementaires,* vol. ix, pp. 202 *et seq.* National Assembly, session 29 Sept., 1789) recommended a direct tax, equivalent to three days labor in local money value, for participation in the primary assemblies, doubled this for membership in the communal and départemental assemblies, and made membership in the National Assembly contingent upon payment of the famous marc d'argent. Sieyes was still in favor of a voluntary tribute (*Observations sur le rapport du comité de constitution concernant la nouvelle organisation de la France,* pp. 21-22), but he did not debate on the subject.

Direct taxes remained a feature of the franchise qualification in the constitution of 1791, but Sieyes does not seem to have incurred the censure of the radicals on that account. Robespierre attributed the discrimination to the " aristocratic party of the assembly " (*Correspondance,* Michon, G., ed., p. 58, Robespierre to Buissart, early November, 1789), while Marat, writing a year and a half later laid the blame at the door of Mirabeau (*Correspondance,* Vellay, Ch., ed., p. 212, Marat to Millan, May, 1791). As to the very light burden entailed by Sieyes' voluntary tax plan, *vide infra,* chap. v.

[19] *Délibérations,* p. 40; *Quelques idées de constitution,* pp. 1-2. Here he suggests that the new divisions be called " départements."

engrossing the attention of the Committee on the Constitution itself. The members of the Committee, following Mounier's lead, resigned in protest against the adoption of these latter measures,[20] but Talleyrand and Sieyes were both reelected (15 September).

Two weeks later, Thouret read a long report on territorial reorganisation and the representative system, a report full of the abbé's ideas as he had outlined them to the Parisians. The first part, especially, is predominantly Sieyesian.[21]   Enumerating the evils arising from the division of the country into ecclesiastical, military, administrative and judicial units, it proposes the creation of eighty-one départements, carved out, as far as possible, with respect for former limits and ease of communication, and then proceeds to outline further division into communes and cantons, with specifications as to the primary assemblies through which all active citizens would participate equally, but indirectly, in the communal and départemental assemblies, and in the national government. Three days later he brought out his *Observations on the Committee's Report*,[22] explaining and defending the proposed plan.

[20] Mounier, *op. cit.*, p. 49.

[21] Thouret's full report is to be found in the *Archives Parlementaires*, vol. ix, pp. 202 *et seq.*, National Assembly, session 29 Sept., 1789. I have compared this report for the Committee with Sieyes' *Quelques idées de constitution.* There are many similarities, as, for instance, in the size, names and character of the divisions, and the plan for indirect representation by means of communes, départements and a national assembly. These show, beyond a doubt, his great influence on the preparation of this important document. Years later, when Mignet asked him if he was the principal originator of the départements, Sieyes replied: "The principal one! Better than that, the only one!" (Mignet, F. A. M., *Portraits et notices*, p. 78). The first part was probably written by Sieyes. It has his terse, epigrammatic style and he allowed it to be printed in the Ebel and Oelsner edition of his works. His contemporaries credited it to him (Duquesnoy, *Journal*, vol. ii, p. 343; *Moniteur*, editorial, 29-30 Oct., 1789; Barère, *Mémoires*, vol. i, p. 304).

[22] *Observations sur le rapport du comité de constitution, concernant la*

Antraigues and Mirabeau attacked his départemental redivisions as too " geometrical," and as depriving the people of the direct choice of their representatives,[23] but its main idea held. On 19 October, the Assembly accepted the Committee's plan as a basis of discussion; 11 November, it was voted that France be redistricted into from seventy-five to eighty-five départements; the following day it was decreed that every département should be divided into districts, and the cantonal subdivision was decreed on 16 November. Throughout November came the decrees establishing the representative system substantially as outlined by Sieyes and the Committee, and the definite number of eighty-three départements was fixed by the decree of 15 January, 1790.[24] Sieyes must have been highly satisfied to see his labor fructify, but it was his last really constructive work in the National Assembly.

Dogmatic and dictatorial in temperament, he was too

nouvelle organisation de la France (Versailles, 2 Oct., 1789). He was not altogether satisfied with the representative system outlined in the committee's report, and suggested a more direct plan of voting (pp. 48-51), but there is no criticism of the départemental plan.

[23] *Joint du Jour.*, vol. iv, pp. 15-16, session 3 Nov., 1789, for Mirabeau's speech; Antraigues, *Observations sur la nouvelle division du royaume, passim.* Aulard (*Etudes et leçons*, vol. vii, pp. 60-62, 69-73, 80) criticizes Sieyes for his rigid, geometrical designs. But the abbé was careful to explain that his outline scheme of perfectly square cantons, communes and départements was only an ideal form that would yield, wherever necessary, to the exigencies of special situations (*Observations sur le rapport du comité*, p. 4). The committee's plan was defended by Thouret, Desmeunier, and others during the November sessions.

[24] *Point du Jour.*, vol. iii, du mardi, 20 Oct., 1789; vol. iv, pp. 135, 144, 183, 195, 209, 211-215, 278; *Arch. Parl.*, 1 série, vol. xi, p. 716. But Sieyes' activity in connection with this project ceases, so far as one can tell, after 2 October, 1789. He does not speak or write on it during the ensuing months, and he was not on the Committee of Division which the Assembly appointed in January to see to the application of the plan. Most influential at the beginning he undoubtedly was, but that influence did not continue to make itself felt.

prone to believe in his own political infallibility. " Politics is a science which I believe I have mastered," he told Dumont one day, and Gouverneur Morris heard him descant on government " with insufferable complacency " at Madame de Staël's salon.[25]   Such an attitude was scarcely conducive to popularity.

The first hints of revolt against this oracular person came in the form of criticisms levelled at his abstruse profundity. This was the burden of the adverse comment on his Declaration of Rights, attacks bitterly resented by the abbé.[26]   But at the same time a more specific grievance against him was found.

The cahiers had shown marked favor to the idea of suppressing the tithes, and when, on the night of 4 August, the feudal system received its death-blow, the Assembly decreed in principle their general redemption.   It was not enough. On the eighth, Lacoste, backed by Alexander Lameth, began an agitation for their complete suppression, without indemnity.[27]

Sieyes, either through a sense of justice, or through a resurgence of what Mirabeau called his " ecclesiastical spirit," [28] immediately threw all the influence he possessed

[25] Dumont, *Souvenirs*, p. 63, note; Sparks, G., *The Life of Gouverneur Morris*, vol. i, p. 353. Extract from Morris' diary, 25 Jan., 1791.

[26] Desmeuniers, cited by Mirabeau in the *Courrier de Provence*, vol. ii, no. 22, p. 21, 1-3 Aug., 1789; *Révolutions de Paris*, vol. i, no. 6, p. 36; Duquesnoy, *Journal*, pp. 291, 300; *Procès-Verbal de l'Assemblée Nationale*, vol. ii, p. 6, 27 July, 1789, report of the Bishop of Bordeaux for the Committee of the Constitution; Chénier, A., *Oeuvres*, p. 88. " On la trouve trop métaphysique," wrote Chénier of Sieyes' Declaration of Rights. *Cf.* the preface to one of the editions of his Declaration of Rights (pp. 1-16). It is an almost malevolent riposte. Everything he has done, he asserts, has been criticized as metaphysical.

[27] Viallay, A., *Les Cahiers de doléances du tiers état aux états généraux*, pp. 226-229.

[28] *Courrier de Provence*, vol. ii, no. 27, c. 12 Aug., 1789. ". . . il ait

into the opposition. His attacks on this project culminated in his speech of 10 August.[29] Interspersing his remarks with the scathing epigram, "they wish to be free and they do not know how to be just," he argued that the suppression of the tithes would redound not at all to the benefit of the people as a whole, but would be a gift to the landed proprietors. Better by far to make them redeemable and use the money thus to be obtained for tiding over the present financial crisis.[30] His efforts were vain. On 11 August the Assembly decreed the suppression of the tithes.[31]

The effect upon the abbé's popularity was most unfortunate. He had not argued against their elimination, only against their non-redemption, but that made no difference. A storm of criticism broke over his head,[32] and reflections

adopté sur les dîmes un système ou l'on a cru voir l'esprit ecclésiastique plutôt que l'esprit national " (p. 9).

[29] *Procès-Verbal*, vol. iii, pp. 22 *et seq.*, "Opinion de M. l'Abbé Sieyes sur l'arrêté du 4, relatif aux dîmes, prononcé le 10 août, à la séance du soir." It is also given in the *Moniteur*, vol. i, no. 39, 10 Aug., 1789. No. 36, 6-7 Aug., 1789, gives a preceding speech by him. The *Point du Jour.*, vol. ii, pp. 50 *et seq.*, mentions only his speech of 10 August.

Sieyes, as well as Mirabeau, had been outspoken against the violent proceedings of the Assembly on the night of 4 August. . . Dumont, E., *op. cit.*, p. 147; Mousset, A., *Un Témoin ignoré de la révolution, etc.*, p. 67. Le comte de Fernan Nûnez à Floridablanca, 16 août, 1789.

[30] The king, in his address to the Assembly, 18 Sept., 1789, used the same arguments as those put forward by Sieyes (*Archives Parl.*, vol. ix, pp. 29-30).

[31] Vialay, *op. cit.*, p. 232. The Assembly was moving steadily toward the abolition of the Church's power and wealth. On 2 November, 1789, it decreed that "tous les biens ecclésiastiques sont à la disposition de la nation" (*Point du Jour.*, vol. iv, p. 32, session 2 Nov., 1789). The decree suppressing the tithes was made final in the following April (*Moniteur*, vol. ii, no. 105. National Assembly, session 14 April, 1790). The infeudated tithes were declared redeemable. The method of redemption was to be thereafter established by the Assembly.

[32] In pamphlets, such as that of Guffroy, A. B. G., *Lettre en reponse aux observations sommaires de M. l'Abbé Sieyes*, or Lenglet, M., *Du Domaine national*. Mirabeau's journal, the *Courrier de Provence*, at-

upon the "accursed robe" multiplied.[33]   He recognized, with open bitterness and chagrin, that his stand had cost him his popularity in the Assembly.[34]

Then followed a series of what can only be described as political defeats. His *Project of a Constitution* was submitted to the Assembly on 12 August. Beginning with his declaration of rights, it proceeded to build up, on the basis of indirect representation, a government of two chambers that should control taxation, supervise expenditures, and hold to account all officials of the administration. The king, as head of the executive branch of the government, was to have control of the civil, military and political administration, subject to the aforesaid supervision by the National Assembly.[35]   The plan was not discussed, and the bicameral system was rebuffed by the Assembly. When, in September, the suspensive veto became the great issue of the day, he opposed it vainly. It was decreed.[36]   In January of 1790,

tacked his arguments at great length (vol. ii, nos. 26-27, 8-12 Aug., 1789). See also M. M. . . . *Refutation de l'ouvrage de M. l'Abbé Sieyes sur les biens ecclésiastiques.*

[33] *Moniteur*, 20 March, 1790; Sieyes, *Projet d'un décret provisoire sur la clergé*, pp. 16-18; Oelsner, *Opinions*, pp. 150-151; Vialay, *op. cit.*, p. 231.

[34] Sieyes, *Projet d'un décret*, pp. 16 *et seq.; Notice*, pp. 32-33; Montlosier, *Mémoires sur les assemblées parlementaires de la révolution*, pp. 6-7. Romilly, who met Sieyes that fall in Paris, wrote: "He was, however, when I saw him, greatly out of humor with the Assembly, and with everybody who had concurred in its decree for the abolition of tithes, and seemed to augur very ill of the revolution" (Romilly, Sir Samuel, *Life*, vol. i, p. 78). Staël-Holstein reported to Gustavus III: ". . . il s'est rendu célèbre par le courage avec lequel il a montré à l'Assemblée son profond mépris pour ses délibérations et pour ses membres" (*Correspondance*, p. 144, De Staël-Holstein à Gustavus III, 22 Oct., 1789).

[35] Archives Parl., vol. viii, pp. 424 *et seq.* At this time, Sieyes was willing to grant the king a suspensive veto, a concession that he was unwilling to make a month later.

[36] Sieyes, *Dire . . . sur la question du veto royal, passim.* The suspen-

he read to the Assembly a plan for press censorship.[37] Designed primarily for curbing seditious and violent writings, it contained little that was new. The Assembly ordered that it be printed, and at the same time left it severely alone,[38] while many of the journals attacked it and its author, on the ground that it limited the freedom of speech.[39] It was one of those steps which, taken in good faith, only serve to injure the prestige of the one advocating them.

More rebuffs followed. His *Project for a Provisory Decree concerning the Clergy,* which he put out in printed form instead of presenting it directly to the Assembly, would have made the church a mere adjunct of the government, but no action was taken on it by the Assembly and its main result seems to have been the resolution of the Chapter of the Clergy at Chartres asking the bishop to deprive him of his office as vicar-general.[40] Then came his great struggle for the institution of juries to try all cases, civil and criminal.

sive veto passed on 11 September (Buchez et Roux, *op. cit.,* vol. ii, p. 410). It was then that he, and the other members of the Committee on the Constitution, resigned in protest against that and the single chamber decreed by the Assembly.

[37] *Procès-Verbal de l'assemblée nationale,* vol. xii, 20 Jan., 1790. " Projet de loi contre les délits qui peuvent se commettre par la voie de l'impression."

[38] *Révolutions de Paris,* vol. iii, no. 28, p. 54 (16-23 Jan., 1790); *Moniteur,* 21 Jan., 1790. See also Soderhjelm, A., *Le Régime de la presse pendant la révolution française,* vol. i, pp. 122 *et seq.,* for a very excellent treatment of this law.

[39] See the comments of the *Révolutions de Paris,* vol. iii, no. 29, pp. 17 *et seq.* (23-30 Jan., 1790); *Révolutions de France et de Brabant,* vol. i, pp. 491, 591-592; vol. ii, pp. 130-138; 154, note i. The conservative *Gazette de Paris* sneered at Sieyes' style of writing, and found fault because the penalties were not strong enough (vol. ii, 22 Jan., 1790). For defense of Sieyes, see the *Journal de Société de 1789,* no. xiii, 28 Aug., 1790, article by André Chénier.

In August of 1791, a press law was adopted similar in many ways to Sieyes' project (*Moniteur,* 23-24 Aug., 1791).

[40] *Moniteur,* 20 March, 1790 *et seq.; Archives d'Eure et Loir,* G. 337,

Before the Revolution began, Sieyes had urged the excellencies of a jury system,[41] and in September, 1789, while on the first committee of the constitution, he had drawn up a plan of organisation for the judiciary. The second committee had not agreed with his views, and they were only put before the public in March, 1790.[42] The distinctive feature of this plan was its provision for juries in civil as well as in criminal cases, to be chosen from " eligible " lists of " active " citizens. For the time being, these lists were to be made up primarily of lawyers. It also contained provisions for the organisation of a complete court system, and it showed his devotion to the principle of representation, for not only were lists of jury " eligibles " to be drawn up in every département, but the " national grand jury " for trying crimes of state was to be chosen from among the deputies of the National Assembly.

The debate on the new judicial system was opened by Thouret on 24 March, and much support for Sieyes' plan developed. Clermont-Tonnerre, Robespierre, Roederer and Buzot endorsed it, in whole or in part; Rabaud St.-Etienne told the Assembly that four members of the Constitutional Committee were in favor of it; and Sieyes, speaking in de-

fols. 458-462. " Actes capitulaires du chapitre de Notre Dame de Chartres," 19-21 April, 1790. The record does not show that any such action was taken by the bishop. An interesting letter (dated 18 May, 1790, and reprinted in *L'Intermédiaire des chercheurs et curieux*, vol. xiii, cols. 370-372), by J. B. Ranchoup, a canon at Chartres, tells of the way in which the electors of the département condemned the chapter for its conservatism.

A pamphlet bitterly attacking his proposal was written by a deputy from Nimes, M. De Ricard: *Réflexions sur le projet de décret de M. l'Abbé Sieyes, du 12 fevrier dernier, concernant les biens du clergé.*

[41] *Délibérations à prendre*, p. 39.

[42] *Arch. Parl.*, série I, vol. xii, pp. 249-258. " Aperçu d'une nouvelle organisation de la justice et de la police en France." A copy of this pamphlet is in the Archives Nationales, A. D. xviii, a. 63. Dated March, 1790.

fense of his plan, was enthusiastically received. Nevertheless, it was not accepted. The Assembly, swayed by the able arguments of Duport, Thouret and Tronchet, rejected juries in civil cases and turned to the rival plan put forward by Duport.[43] So another of the abbé's projects went down to defeat.[44]

From May, 1790 on, Sieyes took comparatively little part in the activities of the Constituent. Honors were paid to him as one of the founders of French liberty; [45] Mirabeau, in the session of 20 May, spoke of his silence and inactivity as a " public calamity; " [46] on 8 June he was elected president of the Assembly; [47] his position and reputation classed him

---

[43] *Moniteur*, 5 April, 1790 *et seq.*, particularly the debates of 7, 8, 28, 29, 30 April. See also Lebegue, E., *La Vie et l'oeuvre d'un constituant—Thouret*, pp. 220-221; Colfavru, J.-C. " L'Institution du jury en matière civile," in *La Révolution française*, vol. i, 1881, pp. 450, 466-467; Desjardins, A., *Sieyes et le jury en matière civile*, pp. 6-7, 10-12. The Jacobins were strongly supporting civil as well as criminal juries (Fribourg, A., " Le Club des Jacobins en 1790 d'après de nouveau documents," in *La Révolution française*, vol. 59, 1910, p. 532, procès-verbal, séance 30 Avril, 1790, au soir).

[44] Although some remnant was saved. The Assembly adopted Sieyes' views as to keeping the appointment of judges free from royal control, and as to limiting the time available for appealing cases (*Moniteur*, vol. ii, nos. 127-128, 217, sessions of 6, 7 May, and 4 August, 1790). See the speeches by Charles de Lameth and Thouret and the subsequent decrees.

[45] May 12, 1790, at the banquet of the Society of 1789, of which he was a member (Challamel, *op. cit.*, p. 425). On 18 June, a bust of Sieyes was installed there, with much oratory (*Ibid.*, p. 429; Perroud, Cl., " Quelques notes sur le club de 1789," in *La Révol. franç.*, vol. 39, p. 260, Sept., 1900). See also the *Moniteur*, 19 June, 1790, for the demonstration by the committee of the quarter where he lived.

[46] " Un homme dont je regarde le silence et l'inaction comme une calamité publique " (*Moniteur*, 21 May, 1790). As to the possible arrière-pensée of Mirabeau, see Barère, *Mémoires*, vol. i, p. 311; Camille Desmoulins in *Révols. de France et de Brabant*, vol. iii, no. 28, pp. 186-190; and the letter of Merlin de Thionville in the *Moniteur*, 12 ventôse, III (2 March, 1795).

[47] *Moniteur*, 9 June, 1790. He pled ill-health as a reason for his

with the moderate patriots.[48]   But during the latter half of
1790, when the civil constitution of the clergy was being
adopted, and the Assembly was busy with the finances and
the development of its plans for the judiciary, his voice was
never raised.[49]

Indeed, there is little to be said of his activities for the
remainder of the Constituent.   " Sieyes is dead," chanted a
contributor to Camille Desmoulins' journal, and Camille referred to the abbé as the " seven-branched candlestick of the
Assembly, whose light has been withdrawn for more than
a year," [50] a jibe with enough truth in it to sting.   He was
elected an administrator of the département of Paris (3 February, 1791) but did not keep that post for any lengthy time.

reluctance in accepting the honor.   The latter was " a brevet of apostasy,"
snarled Camille Desmoulins (*Révols. de France et de Brabant,* vol. iii,
no. 29, pp. 227-228).

[48] Bacourt, Ad. de, *Correspondance entre le comte de Mirabeau et la
comte de la Marck,* vol. ii, pp. 84-85 (ninth note of Mirabeau to the
Court; 7 July, 1790), and vol. ii, p. 88 (Mirabeau to La March, 7 July,
1790) ; *Révols. de Paris,* vol. v, no. 64, p. 591; *Révols. de France et de
Brabant,* vol. iii, no. 29, pp. 227-228, and no. 38, pp. 649-650.   Camille, to
judge by the tone of his remarks, regarded Sieyes as a kind of lost
leader.

[49] His interest in the Committee of the Constitution seems to have
waned.   A contemporary remarked: " On reproche à l'Abbé Sieyes
d'avoir cessé de développer les mêmes lumières qu'au commencement de
la révolution, dont il a jeté la première pierre." (*Correspondance secrète
inédite sur Louis XVI, Marie Antoinette, la Cour et la Ville de 1777
à 1792,* vol. ii, p. 452. Letter 24, Paris, 12 June, 1790. Also vol. ii,
p. 515. Lettre 13, Paris, 26 March, 1791.) " On pretend que le comité
de constitution est entièrement corrompu. L'Abbé Sieyes n'y pariot que
très-rarement."

Mirabeau sent two notes to the Court in December of 1790, wherein
he analyzed the various powers and influences at work in the Assembly.
He entirely disregarded Sieyes (Bacourt, *op. cit.,* vol. ii, pp. 386 *et seq.,*
notes 46, 47).

[50] *Révolutions de France et de Brabant,* vol. v, no. 62, p. 441, and vol.
vi, no. 69, p. 151.

His refusal to be considered for bishop of Paris, two days after it had been decided not to elect him, brought a cry of sour grapes from some of the journals.[51] When the question of religious persecution and its regulation in Paris came before the Assembly, he spoke twice in favor of toleration. Talleyrand took the same side, and after a period of debate the orders of the département of Paris that Sieyes had defended were approved by the Assembly.[52] But this was the only real manifestation of influence on his part during 1791, for, although he toyed with the idea of aiding the court party by revising the constitution in such a way as to give the king a more satisfactory position, nothing came of this project.[53]

Shortly thereafter, he was violently attacked at the Jacobins, of which society he was a member,[54] because of his " Declaration to the Patriots of the Eighty-three Départements," which was, in form, an oath to be taken throughout France to support equality, the freedom of the press and a unicameral legislature. Some rather unfortunate expressions in it led to charges that he was attempting to revive the nobility and institute a bicameral legislature. A miniature

[51] *Ibid.*, vol. vi, no. 69, pp. 148-159, 186 *et seq.; Révolutions de Paris,* vol. vii, no. 88, pp. 487-489; *Moniteur,* 6 Feb., 1791 and 14 March, 1791.

[52] *Ibid.*, 19 April, 8 May, 1791; Mousset, *op. cit.,* Fernan Núñez à Floridablanca, 9 May, 1791.

[53] Bacourt, *op. cit.,* vol. iii, pp. 116, 138 *et seq.* (Montmorin à La Marck, 7 Avril, 1791, and the notes de M. Cabanis pour la Cour, 19-20 Avril, 1791).

[54] He was a member of the Breton Club by the first of July, 1789 (Challamel, *op. cit.,* pp. 276-278; Aulard, *Jacobins,* vol. i, introd., pp. 2-3, 8, 15. Buchez et Roux *op. cit.,* vol. ii, p. 36; Barère, *Mémoires,* vol. i, pp. 292-293). In 1790 he was one of the principal men in the Club of '89, which became more and more upper bourgeois (Challamel, *op. cit.,* pp. 391, 419-425. See also Perroud, Cl., " Quelques notes sur le Club de 1789," in *La Rév. franç.* vol. 39, Sept., 1900). In July, 1791, as a result of the affair of the Champ de Mars, he left the Jacobins and helped found the Feuillants, but in the fall of 1791 he went back to the Jacobins (Aulard, *Jacobins,* vol. iii, p. 33, and Challamel *op. cit.,* pp. 291, 320-321).

tempest arose at the club, and was only quieted by Sieyes' rather obsequious withdrawal of the offending document.[55] At the same time that this discussion was raging, came the king's attempt to sever his connections with a political system that had become increasingly hateful to him, and the flight to Varennes startled the country.   Sieyes determined to retreat behind a philosophic silence.[56]   It was a resolution that, as regards active political life, he did not break for well over a year.[57]

[55] There were undoubtedly political intrigues back of this incident.   See the very interesting, though anonymous, *Bruckstücke aus den papieren eines Augenzeugen und unparteiischen Beobachters der französischen revolution*, pp. 108, 110-111.

According to Mme. Roland, Condorcet aided Sieyes in drawing up this oath—*Lettres de Mme. Roland*, vol. ii, p. 301.   Mme. Roland à M. Henri Bancal, Paris, 20 Juin, 1791.

[56] He gives the trouble at the Jacobins and the king's flight as the reasons for his going into retreat.   *Notice*, pp. 36-40.

[57] During July of 1791 he engaged in a letter-controversy (published in the volumes of the *Moniteur*) with Thomas Paine on the subject of monarchical as against republican government.

He was not a member of the Legislative Assembly (1 Oct., 1791-21 Sept., 1792), but that would have been impossible in any event, due to Robespierre's "self-denying ordinance," which excluded all members of the Constituent.

CHAPTER IV

His Place in the Revolution. Convention and Directory

During the stirring events of 1792, when the war against Austria began, and the conflict between king and nation finally resulted in the suspension of the monarch (10 August, 1792) and the election of a national convention to draw up a new and republican constitution, Sieyes remained aloof and retired in the country, a little way from Paris. He was meditating a more remote retreat when he learned of his election to the Convention.[1] His mind filled with somber forebodings, he came to Paris and took his seat on 21 September, 1792. He had been elected by three départements, Sarthe, Gironde and Orne, but chose to sit for the Sarthe, perhaps because the electors of that département had been most assiduous in their efforts to find him and ascertain his acceptance or rejection of the honor which they had conferred upon him.[2]

On 5 October he was elected one of the three secretaries of the Convention and a week later was made a member of the Committee on Public Instruction and also of the Committee on the Constitution. He chose to sit on the latter, but his interests, or his pessimism, precluded any activity in constitution-making.[3] On 4 January, 1793, this

[1] *Notice*, pp. 40-42.

[2] Grégoire, *Mémoires*, vol. i, p. 410; *Moniteur*, 10-11 Sept., 1792.

[3] *Moniteur*, 5, 12 October, 1792; Guillaume, Jas., *Procès-Verbaux du Comité d'Instruction Publique ... de la Convention*, vol. i, p. 365, note 1; Cahen, L., *Condorcet*, p. 469. According to the records in the *Moniteur*, Sieyes took no part in the Convention's discussion of the constitution of 1793.

committee named him as one of its three members delegated to the new Committee of General Defense, a post he held for a little over a month. There, during January, he drew up a report on the organisation of the war department. It was adopted by the committee and presented to the Convention.[4] A storm of opposition developed there and at the Jacobins, and it never went beyond the stage of printing, Barère's proposal being adopted in its stead.[5] Nothing more was heard from the rejected leader. The committee was dissolved on 17 February, and when it was reorganized, late in March, Sieyes, although reelected, refused to go back to it, alleging that he was too busy on the Committee of Public Instruction.[6]

He had been put on this latter committee 28 February. Condorcet was one of its most influential members, but, on 23 May, Sieyes was elected chairman, and during the month of June an educational project previously adopted was discarded in favor of one that was sponsored by, and was, in large part at least, the work of Sieyes.[7]

On 1 June, he, together with Condorcet and Duhamel, be-

[4] Aulard, A., *Recueil des Actes du Comité de Salut Public*, vol. i, pp. 389-391, 455.

[5] *Moniteur*, 26 Jan.–5 Feb., 1793. Sieyes proposed a centralized system for purchasing supplies, a single minister of war, and a "ministère ambulant" to be with the army and act as a check on the general in command. This last is certainly the same idea that was back of the "representatives on mission." This system was adopted by the Convention on the report of Fabre d'Eglantine, who had spoken against Sieyes' project, considered as a whole.

For criticism and discussion of Sieyes' plan in the Convention, see Buchez et Roux, *Hist. Parl.*, vol. xxiii, pp. 400, 420 *et seq.*, and for Jacobin opposition, *ibid.*, pp. 452 *et seq.*, and Aulard, *Jacobins*, vol. v, pp. 12-13. The plan was attacked as being unduly centralized, and as faulty from an economic standpoint.

[6] Aulard, *Com. de Salut Public*, vol. iii, p. 81.

[7] Guillaume, *op. cit.*, vol. i, pp. 366, 466, 502. He remained chairman until 14 June, 1793.

gan publishing the *Journal of Social Instruction,* which was to lead all citizens out of " the labyrinth of political opinions and errors which become more inextricably confused every day." [8] It was devoted in part to expounding the members' ideas on national education, ideas that were soon collected into a definite program.

On 26 June, Lakanal, the reporter of the committee, read to the Convention a plan for establishing a national, primary school system. This project was the embodiment of Sieyes' views on the subject.[9] Within its limits (there was no provision for higher education), it was carefully done, and in an effort to render criticism fruitless the committee revised it between the reading and the printing (1 July), putting it more under the control of the legislature, and expunging ten of its forty fêtes.[10] All was fruitless. Hassenfratz attacked it at the Jacobins as aristocratic and bureaucratic, " the plan of the priest Sieyes, whose perfidy you know." [11] Lequinio and Coupe de l'Oise criticized it in detail. Robespierre moved that a new commission be appointed to draw up a plan for national education.[12] This was done, and so

[8] *Journal d'Instruction Sociale.* This journal had six numbers, running from 1 June to 6 July, 1793. There were several contributions by Sieyes (*vide infra,* chap. vi). The announcement from which the quotation is taken, appeared in the *Moniteur,* 23 May, 1793.

[9] Lakanal and Danou also had a share in its formation, but Sieyes was the leader. He defended the plan vigorously (*Journal d'instruction sociale,* nos. 3, 4, 5, 6), and a few years later specifically claimed it as his own work (*Notice,* pp. 50-51). He was bitterly denounced at the Jacobins as its author (Guillaume, *op. cit.,* vol. i, p. 525, and Aulard, *Jacobins,* vol. v, p. 281, session 30 June).

[10] Guillaume, *op. cit.,* vol. i, pp. 506 *et seq.; Journal d'instruction sociale,* nos. 5, 6, for Sieyes' defense of the plan and explanation of the amendments.

[11] Guillaume, *op. cit.,* vol. i, p. 524; *ibid.,* p. 526, and *Arch. Parl.,* series i, vol. 67, National Convention, session 25 June, 1793, for the feeling against priests at this time.

[12] Guillaume, *op. cit.,* vol. i, p. 528; *Moniteur,* vol. viii, no. 188, session

the Lakanal plan was definitely shelved. Sieyes was not on this new committee, and when the old one was reorganized (6 October) he was among those dropped from it.[13]

What was Sieyes' part in the factious struggles between the Gironde and the Mountain, and where was he during the Terror? Aside from the activities already recorded, he appears but one other time during the early part of the Convention. That was when, on 16 January, 1793, he voted for the death of the king.[14] But there are evidences of subterranean exertions on his part. Without doubt he worked with the Girondin leaders in the Convention.[15] Boyer-Fonfrède, friend of Vergniaud, wrote that " Sieyes, Brissot and Condorcet, our friends, are the only Frenchmen capable of giving us a good constitution," and Lamartine, who had his information from the woman at whose house Sieyes and the Girondins met, outlines his bold plan of action . . . nothing more nor less than the establishment of an armed, republican

2 July, 1793; *Arch. Parl.*, series i, vol. 68, p. 154, session 3 July, 1793. One of the main charges was that it was a clerical attempt to control education. The plan did not eliminate private schools.

[13] Guillaume, *op. cit.*, vol. ii, p. 592, session of the Convention, 7 Oct., 1793. 31 May–2 June the break had come between the Jacobins and the Gironde. Sieyes had been associated with the latter party (*vide infra*) and this may have had something to do with the bitterness of the opposition, though it was not brought up as an argument. Sieyes remarks that his project was censured as a "complete plan of counter-revolution and federalism," and that it suffered because it had not been presented by a member of the Mountain (*Notice*, p. 51).

[14] *Moniteur*, 20, 24 January, 1793. By the simple phrase "La mort," not, as his enemies insisted, "La mort sans phrase." The *Moniteur* gives no other evidence of Sieyes' activity on the floor of the Convention.

[15] Baudot, *Notes Historiques*, p. 37, quotes Paganel, member of the Convention and confrère of Sieyes, to this effect; Dumont, *Souvenirs*, p. 391, puts Sieyes among the Gironde leaders; according to Lamartine, *Histoire des Girondins*, vol. iv, p. 288 (he quotes from Marat, source unnamed), Marat denounced him, together with the Gironde; and Robespierre, if one may trust Barère, *Mémoires*, vol. ii, pp. 279-280; vol. iv, pp. 428-429, told the latter that Sieyes was the "mole of the revolution."

dictatorship which should crush the Jacobins, overawe the masses, and carry the war of liberation into Belgium and Germany.[16]

Beyond showing that he was in league with the Girondins, the evidence is not very satisfactory. Certainly his activities were much under cover, and, darkly as the Jacobins may have suspected him, none ventured to denounce him from the floor of the Convention during those bitter days of '93, when their opponents were being harried out of the land.[17]

Curiously enough, reports of his being in the opposite camp were bruited about during the Terror. An English spy sent most circumstantial accounts of Sieyes' alliance with Robespierre and the Committee of Public Safety. According to him, Sieyes was the originator of a plan to destroy all religion,[18] was the close coadjutor and supporter of Robespierre, and prompted the overthrow of Hébert and Danton. It is a curious story and may have some foundation in truth, but the evidence appears to be somewhat suspect.[19] It is

---

[16] Lamartine, *op. cit.*, vol. iv, p. 194, quote of letter of Boyer-Fonfrède to his father, late 1792. See also pp. 196-197. The group met every night at this woman's house. According to her account, Sieyes also wanted to save the royal family, condemning them to "eternal ostracism' as soon as peace was declared.

[17] Denunciation of the Gironde leaders was frequent during 1793 and 1794, but in none of the diatribes, as recorded in the *Moniteur*, have I found a reference to Sieyes. A possible explanation would be his connection with the Mountain, which is considered in the ensuing text.

[18] It was at this time that Sieyes made the formal abjuration of his faith—*Moniteur*, vol. ix, no. 51. National Convention, session 20 Brumaire, II (10 Nov., 1793).

[19] These reports are given in the *Dropmore Papers* (9 vols., London, 1892-1915), vol. ii, pp. 462-463, 549, 553, 555, et *passim*. The reports published extend from Nov., 1793 to June, 1794. The unpublished reports show Sieyes as trying (22 June-19 July, 1794) to check the break in the Committee of Public Safety and unite the factions in foreign war. Finding this impossible, he vanished (*ibid.*, vol. iii, introduction, pp. 28 et *seq.*, by Mr. Walter Fitzpatrick). I have had no opportunity to examine these later documents, but certainly the earlier ones are in-

probable that Sieyes gave advice to the Committee at different times, but the nature of that advice is far from certain. At all events, he manoeuvred under cover, for nowhere does his name appear in connection with the stirring events of 1794, either during or immediately after the régime of Robespierre. Only late in that year did he again openly participate in public affairs.

On 28 February, 1795, Mallet du Pan wrote from Berne: " The Abbé Sieyes is the most dangerous man produced by the Revolution . . . it would be most unfortunate to see him regain his influence." [20]   He does not say what information had reached him, but it was a fact that the " most dangerous man " was again taking an open interest in public affairs.   He was named a supervisor of the normal school

accurate. On 13 March he puts eight members on the Committee of Public Safety. There were nine (*Dropmore Papers*, vol. ii, p. 549; Aulard, *Actes du Comité de Salut Public*, vol. xi, p. 669). Seven on 27 March, when there were nine (*D. P.*, vol. ii, p. 555; *Comité de Salut Public*, vol. xii, p. 210), and there are other similar mistakes. He has St. Just absent when he was present (*D. P.*, vol. ii, p. 584; *Comité de Salut Public*, vol. xiv, pp. 152 *et seq.*), and makes Sieyes responsible for action in regard to the revolutionary tribunals of the départements that was the opposite of what really took place (*D. P.*, vol. ii, p. 573; *Comité de Salut Public*, vol. xiii, pp. 509-520).

Mallet du Pan's report on the Committee of Public Safety, sent to the Earl of Elgin in March, 1794, does not once mention Sieyes (*Dropmore Papers*, vol. iii, pp. 491-505).

Mr. J. H. Clapham, in a critical commentary ("A Royalist Spy during the Reign of Terror," in the *English Historical Review*, vol. xii, pp. 67-84, Jan., 1897), concludes that they are unreliable, but that, taken in conjunction with other evidence (Tissot, *Hist. de la Revol.*, vol. v, p. 443, and Sainte-Beuve, *Causeries de lundi*, vol. v, p. 189), they may show that Sieyes was sometimes asked to give advice, without being in league with Robespierre, and probably without any such bold schemes as those mentioned by the spy.

Neton (*Sieyes*, pp. 216-224) denies his complicity with Robespierre's party.

[20] Mallet du Pan, *Correspondance inédite de Mallet du Pan avec la Cour de Vienne*, vol. i, p. 127.

of Paris, but soon resigned. He accepted a position as a substitute member of the Committee on Legislation, and used this as an excuse for an unsuccessful attempt to avoid serving on the Committee of Twenty-one, which examined the charges against those accused of treason and other grave crimes of state.[21] In February his apologia, the *Notice,* was published. Although anonymous, it was immediately accepted as his work and the *Moniteur,* in its lengthy review, gave him high praise.[22] All this was evidence of increasing influence, evidence that was powerfully substantiated when, 5 March, 1795, the Convention elected him to the Committee of Public Safety, the great committee that, since 1793, had been guiding the destinies of France.[23]

Through the spring and summer of 1795 Sieyes' activities followed two lines, diplomatic negotiations and internal politics. In the latter he showed himself a strong opponent of the radicals, for he joined the reaction that was evident in late 1794 and in 1795 against Jacobinism and Terrorism. He helped in bringing back the Girondins to the floor of the Convention, and he proposed a severe law, the *Loi de grande police,* with penalties of transportation and death levelled against any who should attempt to subvert the status quo. It was carried in the face of bitter opposition from the extreme left.[24]

[21] *Moniteur,* vol. xi, no. 54, National Convention, session 22 Brumaire, III (12 Nov., 1794); no. 89, session 27 Frimaire, III (17 Dec., 1794); no. 101, session 9 Nivôse, III (29 Dec., 1794); 3 Pluviôse, III (22 Jan., 1795).

[22] *Ibid.,* 27 Pluviôse, III (15 Feb., 1795); Mallet du Pan, *Correspondance,* vol. i, p. 126.

[23] *Moniteur,* vol. xi, no. 168, National Convention, session 15 Ventôse, III (5 March, 1795).

[24] *Ibid.,* vol. xi, nos. 170-171, National Convention, session 18 Ventôse, III (8 March, 1795); no. 185, session 1 Germinal, III (21 March, 1795), *et seq.* See also, Merlin, R., *Merlin de Thionville,* vol. ii, pp. 425-426. This really ferocious law was passed 21 March, 1795, the day of the

At the same time he took an active interest in the new constitution then being formed, despite his assertion that the democratic constitution of 1793 was the " supreme law," " respectable and not to be attacked." [25] He served on two constitutional committees, but the first of these accomplished nothing, and he had been on the other only a little over a week when a decree of the Convention forced him to choose between that and the Committee of Public Safety. He chose the latter,[26] although his interest in the constitution remained. He had a plan of his own, which he communicated to the Committee of Eleven and afterward outlined to the Convention,[27] but his influence on the constitution of the Year III was slight. Attacked by Thibaudeau, whose strictures were palliated, although upheld, by Danou, he saw his plan go back to the Committee of Eleven.[28] There it remained.

popular uprising in favor of the Terrorists (Billaud, Collot, and others) then on trial. Aimed primarily against the Mountain, it could be used against the royalists as well.

[25] *Moniteur*, vol. xi, nos. 187-188, National Convention, session 4 Germinal, III (24 March, 1795).

[26] *Moniteur*, vol. xii, nos. 198, 217, National Convention, sessions 14 Germinal, 4 Floréal, III (3, 23 April, 1795); Aulard, *Com. de Salut Public*, vol. xxii, p. 666. The first constitutional committee, instituted 14 Germinal (3 April), gave way to the Committee of Eleven, 4 Floréal (23 April). The decree of 15 Floréal (4 May) forbade anyone to serve on the Committee of Eleven and on the Committee of Public Safety at the same time.
Sieyes was made President of the Convention (20 April–5 May), despite his attempt to escape by alleging the state of his health and his work on the committees (*Moniteur*, vol. xii, nos. 215, 231, National Convention, sessions 1 and 16 Floréal—20 April and 5 May, 1795).

[27] As to Sieyes' relations with the Committee, see Stern, A., " Sieyes et la constitution de l'an III " (*La Révol. franc.*, vol. xxxix, Oct., 1900) and Danou's speech to the Convention (*Moniteur*, 11 Thermidor, III— 29 July, 1795). Sieyes spoke on the constitution and outlined his plan 2 Thermidor III—20 July, 1795 (*ibid.*, vol. xii, no. 307).

[28] *Ibid.*, vol. xii, nos. 308, 311, Nat'l. Convention, session 2 Thermidor, III (20 July, 1795).

One of its features, the constitutional jury, which was to guard the constitution against the legislature, was fought out on the floor of the Convention and decisively rejected.[29] Its other plans, including that for a unicameral legislature and a body of tribunes, died a natural death.[30] Observers reported that Sieyes was much out of patience with the new constitution,[31] but at least he could solace himself with his accomplishments on the Committee of Public Safety.

As has been stated, Sieyes entered that committee on 5 March, 1795. He served four months, then left (3 July), ineligible for one month, but as was customary he was re-elected (2 August), and remained until the Directory took over the government on 2 November.[32] Going immediately into the diplomatic section, he began to interest himself in foreign affairs, and, from March to October, a group composed principally of Sieyes, Merlin of Douai, Reubell, Treilhard, Boissy d'Anglas and Louvet directed the foreign policy of France.[33]

[29] *Moniteur*, 7 Thermidor, III (25 July, 1795) *et seq.* For its rejection, see the Nat'l. Convention, session 25 Thermidor, III (12 Aug., 1795).

[30] The most that can be said for the influence of Sieyes' project is embodied in Danou's tactful remark that several of its features had " some resemblance to those outlined in our plan" (*Moniteur*, 11 Thermidor III (29 July, 1795), Nat'l. Convention, session 2 Thermidor).

I cannot understand Bourgeois' reference to Sieyes as the originator of the constitution of 1795—*Manuel historique de politique étrangère*, vol. ii, pp. 137-138. *Cf.* Aulard, *Fr. Rev.* (Miall transl.), vol. iii, pp. 275, 279, 295-298.

[31] Mallet du Pan, *op. cit.*, vol. i, p. 248. Berne, 12 July, 1795. "... L'abbé Sieyes lui-même est mécontent à beaucoup d'égards de cette constitution qu'il voulait fabriquer tout seul..." See also vol. i, p. 286, letter dated Berne, 23 Aug., 1795.

[32] Aulard, *Com. de Salut Public*, vol. xx, p. 669; vol. xxv, p. 93; vol. xxvi, p. 108; Sorel, A., *L'Europe et la révolution française*, vol. iv, p. 168. All members of the Committee served four months and were then ineligible for one month.

[33] Aulard, *Com. de Salut Public*, vols. xx-xxvi, *passim.*

His activities and their significance will be taken up more in detail in a later chapter. Suffice it to say here that he early became the leader in the peace negotiations with Holland (March-June, 1795). He went to the Hague with Reubell, during May, and secured a treaty of peace and alliance very advantageous to French interests, a treaty by means of which France dominated the Batavian Republic, opening the Rhine, Meuse and Scheldt to French commerce, and obtaining control of the important port of Flushing. It was a step toward ending the tyranny of England and establishing the freedom of the seas, he told the enthusiastic Convention.[34]

This accomplishment gave him a considerable amount of prestige,[35] and, when he went back into the Committee during August, he was in a position to push negotiations for a treaty of alliance and commerce with Spain that would have put that country under the control of her powerful neighbor. Various factors, to be noticed in the chapter on his foreign policy, prevented the execution of this ambitious project, which, like the Dutch negotiations, was directed toward the ruin of England.

Rumor named Sieyes a member and leader of the Directory,[36] that shifting group of five men which, under the constitution of 1795, controlled the executive power for the ensuing four years. He was, in fact, elected by the Ancients (the upper house of the Legislature), but he had also been

[34] *Moniteur*, vol. xii, no. 249, National Convention, session 2 Prairial, III (21 May, 1795).

[35] Ranke, L. von, ed., *Denkwürdigkeiten des Staatskanzlers Fürsten von Hardenberg*, vol. v, p. 95. Gervinus to Hardenberg, Paris, 15 June, 1795.

[36] Constant, Benj., *Journal Intime*, p. 246. Constant to Mme. la Comtesse de Nassau, 29 Oct., 1795. " Sieyes, Merlin de Douai ou Treilhard, la Revellière-Lépeaux et Cambacérès le composeront vraisemblablement, et ce sera le premier qui dirigera tout."

chosen a member of the Five Hundred (the lower house), and this last he accepted, rejecting the great honor. Carnot was elected in his place.[37]

Once more the leader relapses into silence, and his career becomes difficult to trace. The Directory made him a member of the newly created Institute of Arts and Science,[38] and he was made a member of a temporary financial committee of the lower house.[39] Then the shadows close down, and, for a year and a half there is little of importance to be recorded. In April, 1797, a demented priest, Poule by name, attempted to assassinate him. It was the talk of Paris, and the Five Hundred resounded with tributes to his fame, and denunciations of Royalists and Jacobins. The excitement soon died away.[40]

[37] Debidour, A., *Recueil des actes du Directoire exécutif*, vol. i, pp. 1-3; *Moniteur*, vol. xiii, nos. 45, 46. Ancients and Five Hundred, sessions 10, 11, 16, Brumaire, IV (1, 2, 7 Nov., 1795). In his letter of declination, he asserted that his post in that body absorbed all his energies and that he did not believe the interest of his country called to the Directory a man who "depuis le commencement de la révolution a été constamment en but à tous les partis, à tous sans distinction." A certain amount of pique is evident here. Mallet du Pan suggested that his refusal was due to his desire to act as the power behind the government (*op. cit.*, vol. i, p. 361). Probably it was a combination of health, wounded vanity and dislike of the Constitution of the year III.

According to Carnot (*Réponse à Bailleul*, p. 151), Sieyes also refused the Ministry of Foreign Affairs.

[38] Debidour, *op. cit.*, vol. i, pp. 93-94, session 29 Brumaire IV (20 Nov., 1795). His place was in the division of Political Economy under the second class—Moral and Political Sciences.

[39] On 6 December, 1795. This committee had its eye on the sad state of financial affairs, but it reported nothing of importance. (*Moniteur*, vol. xiii, nos. 83, 85, 95, sessions 15, 17, 29 Frimaire, IV (6, 8, 20 December, 1795). On 29 Frimaire, Sieyes, in the name of the committee, requested the creation of a new committee of nine members. It was decreed and Sieyes' activity in this connection ceased.

[40] Saint-Martin, J., "Un Attentat contre Sieyes" in *La Révolution française*, vol. 50, March, 1906; *Moniteur*, vol. xvi, nos. 203, 205, 207.

It was in the autumn of that year, at the end of the first Italian campaign, that Bonaparte manifested a flattering interest in the silent theorist. He wrote to Talleyrand, submitting some constitutional ideas to be criticized by Sieyes, and expressed the fervent hope that Sieyes would come to Italy to help him construct a real constitution for that peninsula.[41] The incident had no further development, save perhaps the outspoken admiration for the Corsican evinced, a month or so later, by the recipient of this pat on the back.[42]

As Sieyes had been eager to persecute the Left in 1795, so he now showed a willingness to crush all signs of reactionary tendencies. The coup d'état of 18 Fructidor, V, (4 Sept., 1797), was made an excuse for persecution of the royalists by the Five Hundred. A committee of which he was a member was appointed.[43] On 16 October, Boulay de la Meurthe made for this committee a positively venomous report, inveighing against all privilege and recommending that the nobility be entirely disfranchised and expelled in toto from France.[44] Considerable opposition developed, and

Five hundred, sessions 22-23 Germinal, V (11-12 April, 1797). The would-be assassin, who was from Provence, asked for a loan of money from his fellow Provençal and was refused. There was no evidence of a political motive.

[41] Iung, Th., *Lucien Bonaparte et ses mémoires* (3 vols., Paris, 1882), vol. i, pp. 479-481, appendix no. xxix. Napoleon Bonaparte to Talleyrand, 19 Sept., 1797.

[42] Bailleu, P., ed., *Preussen und Frankreich von 1795 bis 1807*, vol. i, p. 166. Sandoz Rollin from Paris, 22 Dec., 1797. Speaking of Bonaparte, he says: "Les chefs et les meneurs de ces derniers sont devenus ses admirateurs, et le dur et inflexible Sieyes est du nombre."

[43] *Moniteur*, vol. xvii, no. 8. Five Hundred, séssion 4 Vendém. VI (25 Sept., 1797). On the motion of Boulay de la Meurthe. Jean De Bry, Boulay, Sieyes and four others were on it. Sieyes had also been on a similar committee of five appointed 19 Fructidor (*ibid.*, vol. xvi, no. 354, Five Hundred, session 19 Fructidor).

[44] *Ibid.*, vol. xvii, nos. 27, 28, Five Hundred, session 25 Vendém., VI (16 Oct., 1797). The style is Sieyesian—"Qu'est-ce en effet que la

the plan was withdrawn; another, for disfranchisement only, was substituted and decreed.[45]

But, by and large, Sieyes took little part in the proceedings of the Five Hundred, and it must have been a pleasure to him to be offered, as he was in the spring of 1798, the post of envoy extraordinary to Berlin.

French affairs seemed prosperous in May of that year. At peace with all save England, girded with allies in Switzerland, Italy, Spain and Holland, enlarged by the addition of Belgium which had been wrested from Austria at Campo Formio, the Republic and its Directory might have appeared equipped to bid defiance to the world. But, to those who could read them, the signs of the times were by no means auspicious. French possession of the Left Bank of the Rhine was far from definitely settled. The negotiations at Rastadt (begun 16 Dec. 1797), for the indemnification in Germany of the princes dispossessed on the Left Bank, were still dragging their weary length along, rife with the possibilities of complication. Furthermore, Talleyrand, the French foreign minister, was seriously alarmed by the threat of a new coalition against the struggling Republic.[46]

République ou la chose publique c'est la chose de tous les citoyens, de tous les volontés, de tous les intérêts, de tous les droits à une volonté, à un intérêt, à un droit commun et souverain. La République est donc essentiellement fondée sur la souveraineté du peuple, sur la loi ou la volonté générale, sur la liberté ou l'indépendance naturelle, etc." How far he contributed to its formulation is, of course, doubtful, but his coöperation may be safely assumed.

[45] *Ibid.*, vol. xvii, nos. 28-32. Five Hundred, sessions 27-29 Vendémiaire (18-23 October).

Sieyes was President of the Five Hundred, 1 Frimaire—1 Nivôse VI (21 Nov.–21 Dec., 1797).

[46] Pallain, G., ed., *Le Ministère de Talleyrand sous le Directoire*, p. 228. Talleyrand au citoyen Treilhard à Berlin, 3 Floréal, VI (22 April, 1798). See also the despatches on pp. 228-229, note 1. Talleyrand feared an Austro-Prussian alliance, plus the possibility of a northern coalition— England, Russia and Denmark.

The force of circumstance indicated a Prussian alliance. Three times during the past two years such a proposal had been made by France only to be refused, but the shrewd minister was determined to make a fourth effort. He offered the mission to Sieyes. It was accepted, 7 May, 1798, and, after receiving instructions to seek an offensive-defensive alliance, the new envoy set out for Berlin, arriving there 20 June.[47]

It is not my purpose to take up in this place the ambitious plans and activities to which he devoted himself. They will be discussed in the consideration of his foreign policy. Suffice it to say here that he was not successful. Decidedly non persona grata to Frederick William III,[48] facing the machinations of the foreign courts and Prussia's invincible inclination to neutrality,[49] his hands were tied. At times success seemed to be hovering in the offing, but these periods were of short duration. In October and November he turned toward Vienna, seeking an entente through feelers put out from Berlin,[50] but the effort was fruitless. Gradually

[47] *Arch, Nat'l.*, AFiii, 521 (3358); *Dropmore Papers*, vol. iv, p. 270; *Arch. des Aff. Etran.*, Mém. et Docu., Prusse, vol. ix, fol. 5, and 223, fol. 81, Sieyes to Talleyrand, Berlin, 5 Mess., VI (23 June, 1798).

[48] Bailleu, *op. cit.*, vol. i, pp. 192-193, Berlin to Sandoz-Rollin, 11 May, 1798; *Geheimer Staatsarchiv*, Frankreich, R., xi, 89, 1798, ii, fol. 87, quoted by Guyot, R., *Le Directoire et la paix de l'Europe*, p. 716, note 2; Pallain, *op. cit.*, p. 249, note 1.

[49] *Arch. des Aff. Etran.*, Prusse, 223, fol. 101, Berlin, 22 Mess., VI (10 July, 1798), fol. 123, Sieyes to Talleyrand, 10 Thermidor, VI (28 July, 1798), fol. 202, Sieyes to Talleyrand, Berlin, 18 Fructidor, VI (4 Sept., 1798), fol. 209, Talleyrand report to the Directory, 23 Fruc., VI (9 Sept., 1798); Prusse 224, fol. 139, Sieyes to Talleyrand, 16 Nivôse, VII (5 Jan., 1799); Allemagne, 675, fol. 217, Talleyrand to Jean De Bry (at Rastadt), 27 Fruc., VI (13 Sept., 1798).

[50] *Ibid.*, Prusse, 223, fol. 218, and Prusse, 224, fols. 43, 45, 59, 81, 95, 102, Sieyes to Talleyrand; Bailleu, *op. cit.*, vol. i, pp. 230-231, note of Zastrow (Berlin, 12 Aug., 1798), and pp. 548 *et seq.*, reports of Reusz (Austrian ambassador to Berlin).

It is interesting to note that Sieyes had been perfectly willing to effect

Sieyes became convinced that his services were to be without result; that Prussia, far from wishing a peaceful solution of European difficulties, would openly oppose a general settlement but for fear of compromising itself; and that it would be worse than useless to proffer an alliance.[51] From the middle of November on, his despatches grew more gloomy in tone.

The Second Coalition was forming, and during the winter and spring of 1799 Europe resounded with the tramp of armed men. By the middle of March, hostilities had broken out in Italy and along the Rhine, and Russian troops began pouring over the Eastern borders. French arms suffered disastrous reverses, and the envoy at Berlin was shunned as though he were the plague. On 6 May he wrote to Talleyrand: " Our excommunication is general, and the proscription of anyone daring to have connections with us is sure. The tocsin of French extermination is being sounded at London, at Vienna, at St. Petersburg, and I beg you to believe, citizen minister, that what I tell you I do not dream, but know." [52]

Two weeks later he was officially informed of his election to the Executive Directory of the Republic. On 24 May, at six o'clock in the evening, he left Berlin, and on 8 June, with splendid ceremonial, was ushered into office at the national palace of the Directory.[53]

His election was due to various factors. The Councils had revolted against the tyranny of the Directors and their mismanagement of the finances, and were stung to action by

a reconciliation with Austria in the spring of 1795.—*Arch. des Aff. Etran.*, Autriche, 364, Sieyes to Rayneval, 23 Germ., III (12 April, 1795).

[51] *Ibid.*, Prusse, 224, fols. 12, 28, 73, 145. Sieyes to Talleyrand.

[52] *Ibid.*, Prusse, 225, fol. 69.

[53] *Arch. Nat'l.*, AF111, 15. *Procès-Verbal du Directoire Exécutive*, Executive session, 20 Prairial, VII (8 June, 1799).

the military disasters. They turned to Sieyes. No one but he could govern, or make the Republic prosper, was the predominant thought.[54] Even the Jacobins were for him, Talleyrand lent his support, and when Reubell went out by lot Sieyes came in, despite the opposition of the Directory.[55]

Sieyes returned to a country torn with internal strife, overrun by brigands, depressed by the sad reports from the frontiers; a land that seemed ripe for anarchy, despite the fact that its people had but one desire, peace.[56] What more natural than they should turn to this oracle of perfection, who had never been allowed to extend himself in action, whose counsels had never been tried? If the mind fertile to conceive should be able also to command, a great triumph would be his reward.

Sieyes longed to overturn the unpopular constitution of the year III, and give France a perfect, political organization,[57] but many obstacles were in the way. He set about removing them.

[54] Staël-Holstein, *Correspondance*, pp. 276, 282, Brinckman to the Swedish Chancellor, 9, 21 June, 1799; Bailleu, *op. cit.*, vol. i, pp. 279-280, Sandoz-Rollin from Paris, 31 March, 1799.

[55] *Ibid.*, vol. i, p. 304, Sandoz-Rollin from Paris, 15 May, 1799; Staël-Holstein, *Correspondance*, p. 271, Staël-Holstein to Gustavus III, 11 March, 1799; Mallet du Pan, *Mercure Britannique*, vol. ii, p. 514, no. 16, 10 April, 1799. For Talleyrand's aid, see the " Notes manuscrites de Grouvelle," quote by Vandal, A., *L'Avènement de Bonaparte*, vol. i, pp. 78-79, and Reinhard, Mme. C., *Lettres de Madame Reinhard à sa mère*, letter dated Paris, 18 Nivôse, VIII (8 Jan., 1800). As to the Directory's attitude, *cf.* Lafayette, *Mémoires*, vol. v, p. 54; Barras, *Mémoires*, vol. iii, pp. 401, 413; La Revellière, *Mémoires*, vol. ii, p. 382; and Fouché, *Mémoires*, vol. i, p. 64.

[56] *Arch. Nat'l.*, AF111, 16, 17, Procès-Verbal du Directoire Exécutive, *passim*; *Le Publiciste*, reports from Germ.-Fruc., VII (March–Sept., 1799) ; Roederer, *Oeuvres*, vol. iii, p. 294; Staël, Mme. de, *Des Circonstances actuelles qui peuvent terminer la révolution*, p. 90; Cambacérès, *Eclaircissements inédits*, quoted by Vandal, *op. cit.*, vol. i, p. 63.

[57] Aulard, " Sieyes et Talleyrand . . . Constant et Barras," in *La Révolution française*, vol. 73, Oct.–Dec., 1920, pp. 304, 307, 312; Gaëte,

The Directory and the Councils were at odds. The former's position was precarious, and the new Director found himself unable to dominate his associates on that body. " What men! " he exclaimed one day, after a turbulent session.[58] This situation could not last, and, the 28-30 Prairial (16-18 June), the Legislative Corps, with Sieyes' complicity, executed a kind of coup d'état, forcing out Treilhard, Merlin and La Revellière-Lepeaux, and replacing them by Moulin, Gohier and Roger-Ducos, the last of whom, at least, was directly under Sieyes' influence.[59] Already the constitution lay within the shadows of oblivion, and the new leader prepared for the next step. He was now comparatively untrammeled by his fellow-Directors, for Moulin and Gohier were mediocre men, and Barras seems to have given little heed to passing events, being absorbed in his personal pleasures.

But the path was not an easy one. The Jacobins, who had gained strength, as always, in the hour of the country's misfortune, soon repented the support that they had given. Sieyes did not measure up to their standards, and, as their power increased through the summer of 1799, they began to attack.[60] Sieyes was accused of royalism [61] at their new

Duc de, *Mémoires*, vol. i, pp. 40-41; Jourdan, Marechal, " Notice sur le 18 Brumaire," in *Carnet Historique*, vol. vii, p. 162, Feb., 1901; Delbrel, " Le Dix-huit Brumaire," in *La Révolution française*, vol. xxv, pp. 173-174, 1893; Bailleu, *op. cit.*, vol. i, p. 424, Roux letter, 18 June, 1799.

58 Gaëte, *Mémoires*, vol. i, p. 43.

59 There is no doubt of Sieyes' complicity. " J'ai chassé du temple," he told Sandoz-Rollin, " à l'exemple de notre Seigneur, ceux qui vendaient, trafiquaient et deshonaraient la République " (Bailleu, *op. cit.*, vol. i, p. 308); *cf.* Staël-Holstein, *Correspondance*, pp. 282-291, Brinckman to the Swedish Chancellor, 21 June, 1 July, 1799, and La Revellière, *Mémoires*, vol. ii, pp. 391-392.

60 Staël-Holstein, *Correspondance*, pp. 299-302, Brinckman letter, 19 July, 1799; Mallet du Pan, *Mercure Britannique*, vol. iii, p. 457, no. 23, 25 July, 1799; *Journal des Hommes Libres*, 19, 26 Messidor, VII (7, 17, July, 1799).

club, where they professed the doctrines of 1793, and vicious assaults upon Talleyrand were probably responsible for that minister's retirement (20 July, 1799). " The worst lot that can fall to a man," said Sieyes, " is to be a Director of the French Republic." [62]

He struck back vigorously. In speeches on the Champ-de Mars, delivered on the occasion of national holidays, he assailed the radicals. " Their aim," he cried, " is to govern, at whatever cost. Frenchmen, you know how they govern! " [63] By the middle of August, the Directory had closed the Jacobin Club in the Salle du Manège; it then proceeded to suspend eleven Jacobin journals and urge a press law,[64] and the re-

They opened clubs and put through the Legislature a law of hostages and a forced loan. *Cf.* Boulay de la Meurthe, *Le Directoire et l'expédition d'Egypte,* pp. 163-164, and Cornet, M. A., *Notice Historique sur le 18 Brumaire,* pp. 6-7.

[61] Boulay de la Meurthe, *Life,* p. 72.

Was Sieyes considering a return to monarchy at this time? Cambacérès asserts that Sieyes entered into negotiations with the duc d'Orléans (*Eclaircissements,* quoted by Vandal, *op. cit.,* vol. i, pp. 119-120)'; Fouché states that Sieyes opposed the son of Egalité, but was favorable to the Duke of Brunswick (*Mémoires,* vol. i, pp. 70-71). Rumors as to this latter are reported by several writers (*cf.* Barras, *Mémoires,* vol. iii, p. 573; Roederer, *Oeuvres,* vol. iii, p. 449; Bourrienne, *Mémoires,* vol. iii, p. 43). Mention is also made of a Spanish prince (Lavalette, *Mémoires,* vol. i, p. 369), and of negotiations with the King of Prussia for a foreign prince (Jourdan, "*Notice*" in *Carnet Historique,* vol. vii, p. 162, Feb., 1901; and Lafayette, *Mémoires,* vol. v, p. 58). Cambacérès makes his statement as a fact. The others are only rumors. If Sieyes did entertain such notions, it seems probable that his object was to find a figure-head for the government, a " Great Elector," whose presence would mitigate European hostility. But the whole affair is very much in the shadow.

[62] Bailleu, *op. cit.,* vol. i, p. 322, Sandoz-Rollin from Paris, 15 Aug., 1799.

[63] *Moniteur,* 26 Thermidor, VII. Speech on the anniversary of 10 August.

[64] *Journal des Hommes Libres,* 28, 29 Ther., VII (15-16 Aug., 1799); *Arch. Nat'l.,* AF*III, 16, Procès-Verbal du Directoire Exécutive, session 17 Fruc., VII (3 Sept., 1799); *Moniteur,* 19 Fruc., VII (5 Sept., 1799).

morseless Sieyes ousted Bernadotte (who was suspected of
being in league with the Jacobins) from the ministry of
war.[65]

In vain the Jacobins in the Five Hundred raged against
the government. " A coup d'état is preparing," cried Briot,
. . . " They want to deliver up the Republic to its enemies
. . . and perhaps the directors of public calamities have a
treaty of peace in one pocket and a constitution in the
other." [66] Their proposals to declare the country in danger,
and to punish with death anyone proposing or accepting a
peace that tended to modify the constitution or dispose of
French territory, designs attributed to Sieyes, were defeated,
and they came out of the mêlée with diminished prestige.[67]

But though he had worsted the radicals they remained very
troublesome, and Sieyes' plan of constitutional revision did
not prosper. To carry it through, a sword was necessary,
for the army was the only real power left in France. That
sword was hard to find. Joubert was his first choice,[68] but

[65] Staël-Holstein, *Correspondance*, p. 328, Brinckman letter, 19 Sept.,
1799; Cambacérès, *Eclaircissements*, quoted in Vandal, *op. cit.*, vol. i,
p. 189. *Cf.* the correspondence relating to Bernadotte's fall as published
in Iung, *Lucien Bonaparte*, vol. i, p. 244, note, and Gohier, *Mémoires*,
vol. i, pp. 140 *et seq.*

Bernadotte went out on 14 September and, according to the *Observateur
Politique* of 30 Fructidor VII (16 Sept., 1799), many citizens left Paris
in fear of a coup d'état. During these days, Sieyes' courage amazed his
friends (Cambacérès, *Eclaircissements*, quoted in Vandal, *op. cit.*, vol.
i, p. 123).

[66] *Moniteur*, vol. xx, no. 352. Five Hundred, session 17 Fruc., VII
(3 Sept., 1799). " Dans les Conseils, surtout dans celui des Cinq-Cents,
il y a une fermentation violente dont les Directeurs, et Sieyes particulièrement ont beaucoup à craindre."—(Staël-Holstein, *Correspondance*,
p. 323, Brinckman letter, 5 Sept., 1799).

[67] Cambacérès, *Eclaircissements*, quoted by Vandal, *op. cit.*, vol. i,
p. 194.

[68] Lafayette, *Mémoires*, vol. v, pp. 122-124; Fouché, *Mémoires*, vol. i,
p. 69; Barras, *Mémoires*, vol. iii, p. 430.

Joubert was killed leading the French forces against the Austrians at Novi, and Sieyes was in despair.[69] Both Macdonald and Moreau were approached. They refused.[70] And then, on 13 October, the news reached Paris that Bonaparte, victor in Italy in 1797, leader of the Egyptian campaign of 1799, had landed at Fréjus. " There is your man," said Moreau to Sieyes.[71]

Bonaparte reached Paris on 16 October.[72] It was inevitable that these two should be drawn together. " He is the only man available," said the theorist,[73] and Bonaparte realized that Sieyes was the man with whom he must align himself.[74] On 9 Brumaire (31 October) they agreed to act

[69] *Grouvelle mss.,* quoted by Vandal, *op. cit.,* vol. i, p. 177.

[70] Macdonald, *Souvenirs,* p. 114; Fauche-Borel, *Précis Historique, passim,* Lanfrey, P., *History of Napoleon,* vol. i, p. 316, note 1, declaration taken from Moreau's trial.

[71] Vandal, *op. cit.,* vol. i, p. 233. Baudin des Ardennes heard Moreau say this, according to a family tradition.

[72] There is no doubt that the Directory, due to the military defeats, had desired his return and sent orders to that effect—orders that never reached him. See Vandal, *op. cit.,* vol. i, p. 180, quoting Cambacérès; Barras, *Mémoires,* vol. iii, p. 485; Mignet, *Notices Historiques,* p. 80, for the reprint of a letter sent by Reinhard, Minister of Foreign Affairs, 19 Sept., 1798; Boulay de la Meurthe, *Le Directoire et l'expédition d'Egypte,* pp. 188 *et seq.* Very suspect are the letters reprinted in an anonymous pamphlet (*La Dictatoriat ou lettres transcriptes de Barras, Syeyes, à Bonaparte,* pp. 13-14), which purport to be from Sieyes, at Berlin, urging a coup d'état on Barras and Bonaparte. Their dates alone (24, 28 Fruc., VII—10, 14 Sept., '99) are enough to discredit them, for Sieyes was in Paris at that time, a member of the Directory.

[73] *Grouvelle mss.,* quoted by Vandal, *op. cit.,* vol. i, p. 261. Although Sieyes was hesitant and suspicious. (*Ibid.,* Vandal, *op. cit.,* vol. i, p. 272; Joseph Bonaparte, *Mémoires,* vol. i, p. 77).

[74] *Grouvelle mss.,* Vandal, *op. cit.,* vol. i, p. 258; Jourdan, " Notice ", in *Carnet Historique,* Feb., 1901, vol. vii, pp. 165-6; Napoleon, *Mémoirs,* vol. i, pp. 67, 72. The victories of Massena and Brune, during September and October, made a purely military coup d'état, based on the plea of necessity, much less feasible.

in concert.[75] Roederer and Boulay acted as intermediaries in perfecting the plans for the coup d' état,[76] rumors of which were abroad in Paris three or four days before the event.[77] On 18-19 Brumaire (9-10 November) the blow fell, the recalcitrant legislators were dispersed by show of force, and the Constitution of the Year III was at an end. But it was Bonaparte, and not Sieyes, who played the leading rôle when the time for action came.[78]

The 19 Brumaire was, practically speaking, the last day of Sieyes' political life. A greater than he had appeared upon the scene, and, after seeing his constitutional plans emasculated, the ex-abbé slowly drifted into an obscurity from which he never emerged. This last phase of his life will be treated in a later chapter, and it is now time to consider his relationship to the growth of national consciousness that was one of the outstanding characteristics of the French Revolution.

[75] Boulay de la Meurthe, *Life*, p. 86. Sieyes recounted the conversation to Boulay as soon as Bonaparte left. Iung (*Lucien Bonaparte,* vol. i, pp. 293-295) gives an account of an interview that took place at Lucien's house on the 10 Brumaire, where Bonaparte forced Sieyes to agree to act first and make the constitution afterward.

[76] Roederer, *Oeuvres*, vol. iii, p. 296. According to Grouvelle, the idea of transferring the Councils to St. Cloud was that of Sieyes and his friends, Bonaparte agreeing. (Vandal, *op. cit.*, vol. i, pp. 268-269.)

[77] Staël-Holstein, *Correspondance*, p. 351, Brinckman letter, 8 Nov., 1799.

[78] Sieyes was at St. Cloud on 19 Brumaire, but took no active part. For the anecdotes in regard to him on that day, see Lavalette, *Mémoirs*, vol. i, pp. 376-377; Barère, *Mémoires*, vol. iv, p. 433; Roederer, *Oeuvres*, vol. iii, p. 302. Joseph Bonaparte (*Mémoires*, vol. i, p. 79) and Gohier (*Mémoires*, vol. i, p. 421) assert that Sieyes had a carriage there, ready for flight if necessary. Vandal ("Brumaire," in *Le Correspondant*, p. 800, 10 Dec., 1900) accepts this story.

CHAPTER V

NATIONALISM. SIEYES' CONCEPTION OF FRANCE

WHAT is nationalism? The purpose of this study is not consonant with any lengthy disquisition upon its remote origins, or with any discussion as to the primary importance of the nation concept as compared with the state concept.[1] Let it suffice that out of " nationality " (a group of people with approximately the same language, culture and traditions), and " patriotism " (the love of one's native land), has come what we today know as " nationalism."

Its elements vary according to the circumstances of its existence, but the following are the most general: a consciousness of common social and cultural traditions; a belief in racial unity; a single language; geographic unity and a sense of common economic interest; a belief in political democracy as the best medium for the expression of the national will (vox populi, vox Dei); and a burning devotion to the national state, which, as the result of political independence and full sovereignty, is the visible embodiment of the national soul.[2]

[1] See Barker, E., *National Character and the Factors in its Formation*, pp. 120-124, for his contention that, until the French Revolution, it was the State which preceded and made the Nation.

[2] The above general statements in regard to nationalism are based on a year's work in Professor Hayes' seminar at Columbia University, and on such books as those of Barker (*op. cit.*), Hayes, C. J. H. (*Essays on Nationalism*); Gooch, G. P. (*Nationalism*); Hauser, H. (*Le Principe des nationalités, ses origines historiques*), and others.

The state of mind produced by the mingling of some or all of these elements is what we know as nationalism. It manifests itself as a vivid consciousness of the unique or admirable characteristics of one's nationality, an intense belief in the right of that nationality to a national state, unified and independent, and the demand that all members of that national state shall accord to it their first obedience and their first devotion.

Such is the basis upon which I propose to judge the writings and the activities of the Abbé Sieyes.

The nationalism of this particular theorist and politician is by no means well-rounded or complete. He never spoke or wrote on its philosophy (what French leader of his time did?) ; he had practically no interest in establishing outside of France the principle of national self-determination; nor did he nourish a devotion to the glorious history and traditions of pre-revolutionary France.[3] But a consideration of his views and desires along the lines indicated affords some very significant evidence of nationalist tendencies, and, in some instances, at least, gives evidence of trends of thought that characterized the Revolution.

As I propose to describe in detail the various acts and theories of Sieyes that denote a nationalist spirit, it is necessary to commence with his definition and concept of a nation.[4]

[3] He despised history—"Les prétendues vérités historiques n'ont pas plus de réalité que les prétendues vérités réligieuses," he wrote, in an early manuscript (Sainte-Beuve, *op. cit.*, vol. v, p. 194). *Cf. Qu'est-ce que le tiers état*, pp. 38, 41-42, 64; *Vues sur les moyens*, pp. 1-2, 31, 36-39. He wanted to erase all that had gone before in France, and build up a new and unitary organization (ms. *Economique politique*, quoted by Sainte-Beuve, *op. cit.*, vol. v, p. 193. See also pp. 196-198). But, as will be seen, he did not disregard the value of tradition in stimulating national pride. He merely wanted to date such traditions from 1789.

[4] It is well to state here that Sieyes' nationalist ideas, with exceptions as noted, apply solely to France. There lay his interests, and there centered his thought and theory.

According to Sieyes, a nation is a body of people, equal in rights and duties, living under a common law that is the manifestation of its " general will." [5] But in his discussion of the problems and difficulties of France, especially in 1789, it becomes evident that the nation was more to him than any such abstract conception. It was a living, vital thing. Repeatedly he emphasizes its ability to will and to act, and the necessity of its freedom and independence. Whatever the nation wills is legal, for that will is the law itself; " . . . in whatever manner its desires manifest themselves, when its will becomes evident all positive law (droit positif) becomes null before it, as before the source and the supreme master of all positive law." [6]   Hence the nation by its own act creates all authority in the state. " The fullness of all powers and of all rights belongs to the nation, because the nation is self-sufficient, exactly like an individual in the state of nature. . . . The associates who compose it give it will, force and action." [7]   It acts through its representatives,[8] who are

[5] *Qu'est-ce que le tiers état*, p. 31 : " Qu'est-ce une nation? Un corps d'associés vivant sous une loi commune et représenté pars le même législature." *Préliminaire de la constitution*, p. 34: " La Nation est l'ensemble des associés, tous soumis à la loi ouvrage de leurs volontés, tous égaux en droits, & libres dans leurs communications & dans leurs engagemens respectifs." " Reconnaissance et exposition raisonnée des droits de l'homme et du citoyen," in the *Procès-Verbal de l'Assemblée Nationale*, vol. ii, pp. 19, 23 : " Tous les pouvoirs publics, sans distinction, sont une émanation de la volonté générale ; tous viennent du peuple, c'est-à-dire, de la nation. Ces deux termes doivent être synonymes."

[6] *Qu'est-ce que le tiers état*, pp. 66-70 : " La Nation existe avant tout. Elle est l'origine de tout. Sa volonté est toujours légale, elle est la loi elle-même. . . . La volonté nationale . . . est l'origine de tout légalité." He goes on to distinguish positive law from natural law. The latter, for him, comprised those innate and uncodified rules that are the very axioms of existence, such as the right to life, and to all liberty that is not harmful to others.

[7] *Délibérations*, pp. 32-33. In his argument on the constitution of the year III, he stated that the beginning of political movement in a free

chosen by the majority of the citizens,[9] and who represent not an order or a locality, but the nation as a whole,[10] and it has a right to demand of those representatives that they employ their time to the best advantage, and that they express the national will.[11] Furthermore, the nation cannot abdicate

country "can only be the nation in its primary assemblies" (*Moniteur*, vol. xii, no. 307, National Convention, session 2 Thermidor, III—20 July, 1795).

[8] The nation, acting by means of representative government, was the chief basis of his political theory. It appears again and again in pamphlets and speeches, and was the basis of all his constitutional projects. *Cf. Qu'est-ce que le tiers état*, pp. 51-52, 59-71; *Délibérations*, pp. 11, 39, 65; *Dire sur le veto royal*, pp. 7-8, 16; *Vue sur les moyens*, pp. 126-127; *Arch. Parl.*, vol. viii, pp. 424 *et seq.*

[9] He followed Rousseau in his devotion to majority rule. All his pre-revolutionary pamphlets insist upon it, and he defended it in later projects. His argument was that the will of the majority expressed the general will of the nation. *Cf. Qu'est-ce que le tiers état*, pp. 74-83; *Privilèges*, p. 4; *Vues sur les moyens*, pp. 17-18; *Délibérations*, pp. 63-65; *Procès-Verbal de l'Assemblée Nationale*, vol. ii, pp. 22-23; *Dire sur le veto royal*, pp. 2, 7.

[10] His opposition to local mandates, expressed in *Qu'est-ce que le tiers état* (p. 43), *Délibérations* (p. 64) and *Vues sur les moyens* (pp. 22, 84 note 1), bore fruit, 8 July, 1789, when his motion quashed the threat to make their power binding (*Cf. Point du jour*, vol. i, pt. ii, p. 134, and Chassin, *Cahiers de Paris*, vol. iv, p. 427). He elucidated his theory in his speech on the royal veto, Sept., 1789: "Le député d'un bailliage est immédiatement choisi par son bailliage; mais médiatement il est élu par la totalité des bailliages. Voila pourquoi tout député est représentant de la nation entière. Sans cela, il y auroit parmi les députés une inégalité politique que rien ne pourroit justifier et la minorité pourroit faire la loi à la majorité, ainsi que je l'ai démontré ailleurs." (*Dire sur le veto royal*, pp. 4-5. *Cf.* p. 14.)

[11] *Journal des états généraux*, vol. i, états, p. 53. Sieyes' motion in the assembly of the Third, 10 June, 1789; *Qu'est-ce que le tiers état*, pp. 85-86. "Il faut d'abord, comprendre clairment quel est l'objet ou le but de l'assemblée représentant d'une nation; il ne peut pas être différent de celui que se proposeroit la nation elle-même, si elle pouvoit se réunir et conférer dans le même lieu. Qu'est-ce que la volonté d'une nation? C'est le résultat des volontés individuelles, comme la nation est l'assemblage des individus."

its authority, delivering it up to any individual, group or class, because that authority is an integral part of itself.[12]   In his argument on the constitution of the year III, he pictures the nation as an entity which remains while generations pass away.[13]

The nation, then, is an all-powerful entity, capable of wishing and willing, and indubitably, for Sieyes, France was a nation; one just awakening to consciousness, in 1789, but with an inherent dignity, with aims and a will to express them,[14] with an energetic national character,[15] and peculiarly susceptible to the force of sentiment.[16]

[12] *Vues sur les moyens*, p. 23.   "Une collection d'hommes ne peut pas plus qu'un particulier, renoncer à la faculté de délibérer et de vouloir pour son intérêt," and (pp. 53-54), "Il n'est point d'individu, point de corps qui ne puisse ainsi séparer son intérêt particulier de l'intérêt général; et par conséquent, se rendre injuste, criminel. La Nation seule en est incapable, car son intérêt particulier c'est l'intérêt général lui-même."

In *Qu'est-ce que le tiers état* (p. 74) he answers the argument that each Order should have equal weight in the formation of the "national will," by saying: "Une nation ne peut pas décider qu'elle ne sera pas une nation, ou qu'elle ne le sera que d'une manière: car ce serait dire qu'elle ne l'est point de tout autre. De même une nation ne peut statuer que sa volonté commune cessera d'être sa volonté commune. . . . Donc une nation n'a jamais pu statuer que les droits inhérents à la volonté commune, c'est-à-dire, à la pluralité, passeraient à la minorité. La volonté commune ne peut pas se détruire elle-même."

[13] *Moniteur*, vol. xii, no. 326, Nat'l. Conv., session 24 Thermidor, III (11 Aug., 1795): ". . . les véritables rapporte d'une constitution politique sont avec la Nation qui reste, plutôt qu'avec telle génération qui passe; avec les besoins de la nature humaine, commune à tous, plutôt qu'avec des différences individuelles." His argument here is that a constitution is a matter of evolution and growth, responding to the needs of the nation.

[14] *Qu'est-ce que le tiers état*, p. 61; *Vues sur les moyens*, pp. 3-4, 11, 23, 25-26, 52, 62-63.

[15] *Arch. des Aff. Etran.*, Prusse, 225, fol. 101, Sieyes bulletin # 4, Berlin, 22 Mess., VI (10 July, 1798). The more one follows the lagging negotiations at Rastadt, he wrote, "plus on a lieu de se convaincre que

This "personality" concept was further emphasized by his remarks on the characteristics peculiar to the French people.[17] They had certain excellencies; unlike the Germans, they applied reason to their statecraft,[18] and the "Machiavel-

le Directoire Exécutif n'obtiendra aucun résultat satisfaisant tant qu'il n'aura pas déployé au dehors tout l'energie du caractère national." *Ibid.,* Hollande, 587, fol. 32, Sieyes to Richard, 22 Germ., III (11 April, 1795). Writing of the English machinations in Belgium and Holland, he says: "L'or et l'intrigue britannique agissent fortement, mais le génie de la France et votre activité déjoueront toutes ces tentatives."

[16] *Arch. Nat'l.,* AF, III, 61. Dossier 10, piece 3. Sieyes à Barthélemy, 4 Vendém., IV (26 Sept., 1795) : "On sait ce que peut le sentiment sur une Nation et surtout sur la Nation française. Pendant longtemps il guidera sa politique; il sera penible et douloureux a l'égard de l'Espagne si l'on laisse échapper le seul moment qui puisse lui donner une autre direction."

[17] So far as France was concerned, "people" and "nation" meant to him the same thing. "...du peuple, c'est-à-dire de la nation. Ces deux termes doivent êtres synonymes" (*Procès-Verbal de l'Assemblée Nationale,* vol. ii, p. 23, Declaration of Rights). *Cf. Vues,* pp. 25, 31, 138; *Privilèges,* p. 4; *Préliminaire de la constitution,* pp. 22-23. He used "Patrie" as a term synonymous with the nation, with France as a whole, never with any local significance. "...à la patrie, c'est-à-dire, à la nation"—(*Privilèges,* p. 4). *Cf. ibid.,* pp. 5-6; *Vues,* pp. 118, 143. But his references to "nations" other than France are meager and rather vague. Thus there were the "nations of the north" (*Privilèges,* p. 4; *Arch. des Aff. Etran.,* Prusse, 225, fol. 10, Sieyes to Talleyrand, Berlin, 12 Ventôse, III, 2 March, 1799). He applies the term, indirectly, to Germany as a whole (*ibid.,* mém. et docu., Allemagne 117, fol. 24, "Projet de traité"), and the English were a nation (*ibid.,* also Corr. Pol., Prusse, 225, fol. 25, Sieyes to Talleyrand, 26 Ventôse, III (16 March, 1799). In all such cases the term is used in a general fashion as emphasizing popular characteristics, rather than definitively as in accordance with his own expressed concept of a nation. If Sieyes had had a philosophy of nationalism the case would undoubtedly have been different.

[18] *Arch. des Aff. Etran.,* Prusse, 225, fol. 10. Sieyes to Talleyrand, 12 Ventôse, VII (2 March, 1799). The Germans, he held, were slow-moving, and were guided not by the force of reason but by the force of wills (volontés). The Prussians, in general, were very bad,—deceitful, boastful and treacherous (*ibid.,* Prusse, 224, fols. 17, 139; Prusse,

lian policies [of the enemies of France] were pursued with an attention and a constancy that the French character found difficult of comprehension!"[19]   But they also had many faults. They were self-centered, and, outside of their personal pleasures and private affairs, everything seemed indifferent and metaphysical to them;[20] they were prone to feel instead of think, and to decide questions before understanding them.[21]   His constitutional jury of 1795, designed to safeguard the constitution against sudden and violent attack, was especially suited "to the real needs of la patrie and of the French character.[22]   Thus he demonstrated from time to time that he had a conception of the French as individual among the people of the earth.

The stimulation, the perfection, of unity in this distinct nation was one of the main features of Sieyes' policy, especially during the early part of the Revolution. Again and again he insisted upon the absolute necessity of such

225, fols. 15, 28. Letters of Sieyes to Talleyrand during 1798-1799). The English were a nation noted for their obstinacy (*ibid.*, Prusse, 225, Sieyes to Talleyrand, Berlin, 26 Ventôse, VII, 16 March, 1799).

[19] *Ibid.*, Prusse, 225, fol. 74, Sieyes to Talleyrand, Berlin, 21 Floréal, VII (10 May, 1799).

[20] *Qu-est-ce que le tiers état*, p. 54; *Vues sur les moyens*, pp. 92, 129; *Préliminaires de la constitution*, pp. 4-5—"Il n'est pas d'acte de patience dont le François sache mieux se défendre, que de donner son attention à ce qui ne l'intéresse, ni dans ses plaisirs, ni dans ses affaires particulières. Hors de ses affections privées et de ses habitudes, toute lui semble métaphysique. Essaya de lui prouver que les hommes, pourtant, n'ont été susceptibles de quelque progrès, que pour avoir su écouter et s'approprier des idées nouvelles ; ce raisonnement là même est encore pour lui de la métaphysique. Car tel est le nom dont la multitude qualifie les vérités les plus utiles, jusqu'au moment où, bon gré, malgré, elles se font jour dans toutes les classes de citoyens."

[21] *Procès-Verbal de l'Assemblée Nationale*, vol. iii, p. 30.

[22] *Moniteur*, vol. xii, nos. 323, 326, National Convention, sessions 18, 24 Thermidor, III (5, 11 Aug., 1795). It is only fair to state that these strictures were frequently a direct reaction to the defeat of his plans.

unity.[23] In 1793, after he had seen so many of his projects buffeted about by the National Assembly and the Convention, he wrote: " The most important, the most necessary of all useful engagements is that which links the will of every individual to the common will of the association, that is to say, to the law. There is no necessity for proving this, since to weaken the law would be to weaken the social state, lose all of its advantages, and open the way to all dangers." [24] I turn now to his specific projects that, indirectly or directly, converged toward this end.

First of all, one is impressed by his insistence, in those days when his theories had not yet been subjected to the somber tests of the Revolution, upon the political equality of Frenchmen.[25]

Inequalities of property or occupation [he wrote in his most influential pamphlet] are like inequalities of age, sex, height and so on. They do not effect the equality of citizenship. . . . It is not, then, for the legislator to create any differences of that kind, to give privileges to some, or refuse them to others. The law accords nothing, it protects that which is, up to the point where it begins to harm the common interest. . . . I picture the law as the center of an immense globe; all the citizens, without exception, are at the same distance on the circumference, and occupy equal places.[26]

[23] *Qu'est-ce que le tiers état,* p. 81; *Déclaration des droits de l'homme,* p. 22; *Projet d'un décret provisoire (Moniteur,* 20 March, 1790) ; *Journal d'instruction sociale* (# 5, 6 July, 1793, p. 146).

[24] *Journal d'instruction sociale,* # 5, 6 July, 1793, p. 146.

[25] This theoretical belief in democracy gave way to the realities of the situations that he confronted. None of his constitutional projects would have established an unlimited franchise, and the democratic aspects of his plan of constitution in 1799 were farcical. Sieyes himself would not have recognized any contradiction here, for, as he had said at an earlier date: " True political science is not the science of that which is, but of that which ought to be " (*Ms.* entitled " Economie politique," quoted by Sainte-Beuve, *op. cit.,* vol. v, p. 193).

[26] *Qu'est-ce que le tiers état,* p. 88.

This idea was one of his favorites,[27] and he applied it to participation in political life. The theorist of those early days advocated a representative democracy that was nearly universal in its scope. For him, political rights were not based on property but were inherent in individuals,[28] and he even regretted the " bizarre contradiction " which permitted women to wear the crown and yet denied them the vote.[29]

[27] " Declaration des droits de l'homme ", in the *Procès-Verbal de l'Assemblée Nationale,* vol. ii, pp. 6-7. Here he admits inequality of means but insists upon equality of rights. He says (p. 9), " L'état social n'établit pas une injuste inégalité de droits à côté de l'inégalité naturelle des moyens ; au contraire, il protège l'égalité des droits contre l'influence naturelle, mais nuisible, de l'inégalité des moyens. La loi sociale n'est point faite pour affoiblir le foible & fortifier le fort ; au contraire, elle s'occupé de mettre le foible à l'abri des entreprises du fort, & couvrant de son autorité tutelaire d'universalité de citoyens, elle garantit à tous la plénitude de leurs droits." *Cf. Dire sur le veto royal,* pp. 11-12; *Délibérations,* pp. 11-12, 26, 42. In the latter he suggests that the representatives of the people be seated in an oval or circle, so that none will have an opportunity to claim preëminence or superiority.

[28] *Qu'est-ce que le tiers état,* p. 44: " Les droits politiques comme les droits civiles, doivent tenir à la qualité de citoyen. Cette propriété légale est le même pour tous, sans égard au plus ou moins de propriété réelle dont chaque individu peut composer sa fortune ou sa jouissance."

Délibérations, p. 13: " Ce n'est pas à la *Propriété,* mais à la *Personne* qu'appartiennent les droits politiques."

Dire sur le veto royal, pp. 11-12: " Vous ne pouvez pas refuser la qualité de citoyen & des droits du civisme, à cette multitude sans instruction, qu'un travail forcé absorbe en entier. Puisqu'ils doivent obéir à la loi, tout comme vous, ils doivent aussi, tout comme vous, concourir à la faire. Le concours doit être égal."

Vues sur les moyens, p. 14: " Les vingt-cinq millions d'hommes qui habitent le Royaume sont libres ; comment concevoir que la Nation ne le soit pas ? Si l'esclavage ne peut trouver à se placer sur aucune tête en particulier, comment pourroit-il en embrasser l'universalité ? En général tout Citoyen à qui on ôteroit le droit de consulter ses intérêts, de délibérer et de s'imposer des loix, seroit considéré avec raison comme serf ; le droit de consulter ses intérêts, de délibérer et de s'imposer des loix appartient donc nécessairement à la nation."

[29] *Observations sur la nouvelle organisation de France,* pp. 19-20: ". . . on ne permettroit, nulle part, de les compter parmi les citoyens

To be sure, he differentiated between active and passive citizenship, but the requirements for the former condition were slight. French nationality, legal majority, a year's residence in the constituency, and the payment of a direct, voluntary, yearly tax of three livres. This last, the only real limitation, was meant primarily to bring financial support to the state, and would have excluded only the outcasts of society, and those not interested in political affairs.[30] In fact, Sieyes asserted that the aim of government must be to reduce the non-voting class to the lowest possible number. During 1789-1791 he worked for the enfranchisement of free men of color in the colonies.[31] He desired that the primary assemblies should be numerous, one to every 600 voters, and at least one to every canton. They contained, he believed, the very fountains of the spirit of democracy, and he felt that they should influence as directly as was feasible the national legislature.[32] He urged that they should elect

actifs, comme si la saine politique ne devroit pas toujours tendri à accroître de plus en plus le nombre proportionnel des vrais citoyens, ou, comme s'il étoit impossible à une femme d'être jamais d'aucune utilité à la chose publique."

[30] *Quelques idées de constitution*, pp. 19-20: " Ceux qui ne voudroient pas se faire inscrire & payer cette legère somme, n'auroient pas véritablement envie de venir voter à l'Assemblée; sûrement ils ne songeroient pas même à se plaindre; ainsi point d'inconvénient à cette condition." A rural laborer in France, 1789, could earn nearly a livre a day, and skilled laborers from two to three livres (Levasseur, E., *Histoire des classes ouvrières . . . avant 1789*, vol. ii, p. 386).

[31] *Quelques idées de ·constitution*, p. 21; *Moniteur*, vol. iv, no. 134, National Convention, session 12 May, 1791; Gregoire, *Mémoires*, vol. i, p. 392; Brissot, *Mémoires*, vol. iii, pp. 123, 131; Cahen, " La société des Amis des Noirs," in *La Révolution française*, vol. 50, June, 1906, p. 483.

[32] *Observations sur la nouvelle organisation de France*, p. 17; *Vues sur les moyens*, pp. 124, 127. In his pre-revolutionary pamphlets he advocated two intermediary assemblies between the primary assembly and the National Legislature (*Ibid.*, pp. 126-127; *Délibérations*, p. 24). Only one was provided for in his *Projet de constitution* of 12 August, 1789 (*Arch. Parl.*, vol. viii, p. 425), and it is interesting to note in this

directly the delegations charged with making or revising the constitution.[33]

This was a vision of a state whose citizens acted as a political unit, and this concept is in harmony with the democratic movement that culminated with universal manhood suffrage in the constitution of 1793. It is certainly permissible to consider Sieyes as a forerunner of that movement, even though he took no actual part in it. Of course, such political unity harmonizes with his general theory as to the unification of France, and we now turn to other, and even more direct, manifestations of this idée fixe.

The warfare that he waged against privilege was motivated by his basic theory. It was impossible, he believed, for France to be a real nation, governed by common laws and submitted to a common order, as long as parts of the citizenry enjoyed special benefits. With the favored groups absorbed in their own designs, and blind to the interests of the nation as a whole, there could be no unity of purpose, and the general will, the very basis of the nation's being, was non-existent. The Orders would have to go, so that a real social structure, and a real nation might be established.[34]   Hence came the

connection that the National Assembly voted, 16 November, 1789, " Qu'il n'y aura qu'un degré intermédiare pour les élections entre les assemblées primaires & les assemblées nationales & les assemblèes administratives " (*Point du jour.*, vol. iv, p. 185). He did not state, in 1795, the number of assemblies that he would have, but his plan for the constitution of 1799 contains little indeed about the direct influence of the voters. At no time did he advocate direct election of the national legislature by the primary assemblies.

[33] *Quelques idées sur la constitution*, pp. 10, 30-31; *Préliminaire de la constitution*, pp. 17-18; " Déclaration des droits de l'homme " in the *Procès-Verbal de l'Assemblée Nationale*, vol. ii, art. 32. As late as 1795 he defended the constitution of 1793 because it had been made in the " assemblies of the people " (*Moniteur*, vol. xii, no. 188, National Convention, session 4 Germinal, III—24 March, 1795).

[34] *Qu'est-ce que le tiers état*, pp. 41-42, 59-60, 80-81; *Privilèges*, pp. 9, 24.

blows that were struck with such great effect against the favored classes. And it is to be remarked that the attack was upon the evil, not upon those who were its agents. Sieyes was willing to recognize the members of the upper Orders as citizens, and he looked forward to their becoming again a source of strength instead of weakness to the nation.[35] In the great levelling of privilege that characterized the Revolution, a movement certainly democratic and unifying in its implications, Sieyes stands out a leader.

He was decidedly opposed to the establishment of the powerful municipal bodies that began to appear in increasing numbers after the downfall of the central authority in 1789. As early as July he regarded them as a menace,[36] and in his speech on the royal veto (7 September, 1789) he came out openly against them. " All is lost," he asserted, " if we permit ourselves to consider the municipalities, etc., as so many Republics, united solely by the bonds of force or the need of common protection," and he proceeded to draw a lively picture of a France " cut up by barriers of all kinds . . . a chaos of customs, regulations and prohibitions peculiar to each locality. This fine country will become odious alike to travellers and to its inhabitants." To check this evil, be proposed that a committee be appointed to draw up a plan for municipalities and provinces that would prevent such a catastrophe and permit France " to form a *single whole,* uni-

[35] *Qu'est-ce que le tiers état,* pp. 93, 33, note i; *Délibérations,* p. 15; *Arch. Nat'l.,* C, 27, 188-192, Sieyes' motion of 15 June, 1789, for the Third Estate to constitute itself as representative of the French nation.

[36] *Quelques idées de constitution,* pp. 1-2: " Nous partons du principe qu'il faut à la France entière, une Législation et une Administration communes et uniformes, et aux Municipalités un Conseil et une Gestion, qui remplacent pour les affaires particulières et représentent le pouvoir législatif et le pouvoir exécutif ; de manière cependant que la Constitution libre et particulière de chaque Cité ou Commune, n'usurpe point sur la Constitution générale de l'Etat, et ne gêne en aucune façon la Législation et l'Administration Nationales.

formly submitted in all its parts to the same legislation and a common administration." [37]   He had hoped, he wrote to Clermont-Tonnerre, to see the municipalities eliminated by the establishment of comparatively small provinces and large communes, and since the Assembly at the beginning of November, 1789, had decreed the 44,000 municipalities, he had never ceased protesting against them.[38]   Certain it is that Sieyes had proposed, and the Committee on the Constitution had accepted, his plan for small provinces and large communes; [39] equally certain is it that the Committee, using Sieyes' arguments, had planned to identify the municipalities with the 720 communes.[40]   The plan gave way before the immediate organisation of the municipalities, against which rapid action the members of the Committee protested in vain,[41] but it sufficiently demonstrates Sieyes' opposition to such a decentralizing tendency.   He continued his agitation in 1790, and Boulay de la Meurthe informs us that he came back to it in his constitutional plans for 1799.[42]

Furthermore, he put himself on record as opposed to federalism, being earnest in his warning that France must be a

[37] *Dire sur le veto royal*, pp. 8, 14 *et seq.*

[38] *Moniteur*, 18 Oct., 1791. Letter dated 13 Oct., 1791. Clermont-Tonnerre replied that he knew Sieyes had always abhorred them (*Ibid.*, 7 Nov., 1791. Letter dated 23 Oct., 1791). Sieyes correspondence with Crillon (*Ibid.*, 25, 29 Oct., 1791) shows the same opposition.

[39] *Cf. Quelques idées sur la constitution*, pp. 1, 5-6, and Thouret's report for the Committee on the Constitution (*Moniteur*, vol. i, p. 264, col. 2).

[40] *Cf.* Thouret's report, part 2 (*Moniteur*, vol. i, no. 65, National Assembly, session 29 Sept., 1789) and Sieyes' arguments in his *Dire sur le veto royal*, pp. 8, 14 *et seq.* Duquesnoy remarks that Thouret's report was based on Sieyes' principles (Duquesnoy, *Journal*, 29 Sept., 1789, p. 377).

[41] *Point du Jour.*, vol. iv, pp. 51 *et seq.*, National Convention, sessions 4, 11, 12 November, 1789.

[42] Sieyes, *Projet d'un décret provisoire sur le clergé*, p. 8; Boulay de la Meurthe, *Théorie constitutionelle de Sieyes*, p. 15.

single state, not such an assemblage of little nations as would
be formed under a federal organisation.[43]   " The American
system, which is suitable to a confederation of several states,"
he wrote during July of 1789, " is foreign to France which
should be a single state; and, if it is necessary to say so, I
believe that its only result would be to ruin everything in
France." [44]   In his own country, he believed, it could only be
productive of discord and perhaps of civil war.[45]

   In his scheme for the territorial reorganisation of France,
he assigned certain duties, such as the administration of taxation and of the local militia, to the communal and départemental assemblies, but he stressed his statement that their true
function was not legislative, but that of connecting links between the people and the national legislature.

No one of good sense [he remarks] would ever think that either
of these assemblies could render itself permanent in order to
direct, that is to say, obstruct the true legislature.   The assemblies intermediate between the corps legislative and the gatherings of the people [comices] should, as soon as they have finished
their tasks, disperse, not to meet again until the following year.
Their directors, comparable to what are called today the intermediary commissions of the provincial assemblies, could act as
their agents during that time, never themselves attempting to
exercise any legislative functions.[46]

In connection with this idea, he urged that the primary assemblies be allowed to elect the départemental as well as the
communal deputies, a plan which would certainly have weak-

[43] Sieyes, *Dire sur le veto royal*, p. 8: ". . . La France ne doit être
un assemblage de petites nations . . . ; elle est *un tout*, unique, compose
de parties intégrantes." In connection with this matter, " les faux principes deviennet extrêmement dangereux." His aim was to prevent " le
royaume se déchirer en une multitude de petits Etats sous forme
républicaine."

[44] *Préliminaire de la constitution*, p. 19, note i.

[45] *Ibid.*, p. 8; *Observations sur la nouvelle organisation de France*, p. 46.

[46] *Ibid.*, p. 52. See also p. 39.

ened the communal assemblies, and made those of the départements more susceptible to popular influence.[47] This opposition to federalism was restated in 1791, in a speech defending the Département of Paris against the charge that, by its religious regulations, it was arrogating to itself too much power and thus leaning toward federalism.[48]

Sieyes' connection with the Girondins in 1792-1793 suggests that he may have lost his hatred of federalism by that time. I do not think that this is the case, although the evidence is purely negative. In none of his speeches or writings is there any proof that he ever favored that particular form of government, nor does Lamartine, who had access to sources now lost, suggest that he shared the federalistic ideas of the Girondins.[49] After the Gironde was crushed, in 1793, destruction menaced anyone who could be accused of desiring a federal republic, but no enemy ever brought such a charge against Sieyes.[50] Probably the best explanation of his gravitating toward the Girondins is that he preferred them to the Jacobins as the lesser of two evils in the gloomy days of '93.

[47] The gist of this idea was that " on supprimera en même temps un degré intermédiaire pour la représentation nationale, & on le conservera pour l'ordre administratif, & pour la surveillance qui doit l'accompagner " (*Ibid.,* p. 51).

[48] *Moniteur,* vol. iv, no. 29, National Convention, session 7 May, 1791. " Pour quiconque n'a pas perdu la mémoire, il reste démontré que ceux-là n'ont pas voulu une république fédérative qui ont proposé de diviser le royaume an 83 départements, plutôt qu'en 9 à 10 grandes provinces. . . Toute le monde convient, de reste, que les départements ne doivent pas se permetter de faire des lois, qu'ils ne doivent pas viser à l'indépendance."

[49] Lamartine, *Histoire des Girondins,* vol. iv, pp. 194 *et seq.*

[50] *Moniteur,* 1793-1794. I have studied the accusations levelled by the Mountain, and they were many, with great care. But Sieyes' name does not appear. Desmoulins' *Histoire secrète de la Révolution, ou histoire des Girondins,* which was originally published in 1793, abounds in denunciations of the Girondins by name, but Sieyes' is not mentioned. Clapham (*op. cit.,* pp. 34-35) also notes the lack of such a charge against Sieyes.

CHAPTER VI

NATIONALISM. FURTHER PLANS FOR UNITY. DEVOTION TO LA PATRIE

No one could accuse Sieyes of being a rabid militarist. He shared with the other members of the Third that distrust of the army which was evidenced so plainly in July of '89, when the king was drawing in his troops about Versailles.[1] His plans for the reorganisation of the war department, drawn up in January, 1793, when France was at war with Prussia and Austria and on the verge of hostilities with England and Holland, evidences no interest in the theory of militarism. It is rather an attempt to increase the efficiency of the service itself.[2]

But he ardently desired to see all French citizens united in a great military organisation that should be the basis for defense, and for the preservation of order. Early in 1789 he began to advocate what we today know as universal military training. He sought a more " national " method than had theretofore existed of maintaining the military establishment,[3] which, like taxes, was a contribution that the nation

[1] The army, Sieyes held, should be so constituted that it should never become a menace to the citizens (*Vues sur les moyens*, p. 139). There should never be any relation between it and the maintenance of internal order (*Déclaration des droits de l'homme*, p. 14; *Préliminaire de la constitution*, p. 12, note; *Quelques idées de constitution*, p. 27).

[2] *Vide supra*, chap. iv, p. 49; *Moniteur*, vol. viii, no. 28, Nat'l. Convention, session 25 Jan., 1793.

[3] *Qu'est-ce que le tiers état*, p. 35. " Tout besoin public doit être à la charge de tout le monde et non d'une classe particulière de citoyens, et qu'il faut être aussi étranger à toute réflexion qu'à toute équité pour ne pas trouver un moyen plus national de compléter et de maintenir tel état militaire qu'on veuille avoir."

should make to its own maintenance.[4] The people, then, should hold themselves ready to protect the nation. Without going into minute details of organization, he outlined his plan for the establishment of what he called the " national militia." This was to comprise the whole body of active citizens; it was to be organized under the direct supervision of the communes, but under the final authority of the national legislature; it was to receive military instruction, on Sundays, in each of the cantons; in fact, it was to constitute the reservoir from which should be drawn all the active military forces needed by the nation. " Every citizen is a soldier," remarked the abbé, " and, where society is well constituted, the army in commission is only a detachment of the great national army." [5]   In his plan for national primary schools, he sought to establish a system of military training for the youth of the land.[6]

There is no evidence that he was ever directly responsible for decrees stimulating French militarism, although Carnot and Talleyrand both told Lord Brougham that Sieyes should be given exclusive credit for suggesting what developed into the French National Guard.[7] But it is obvious that he considered his plan for military training as a necessary part of that national reorganization to which he was so greatly devoted.

[4] *Quelques idées de constitution*, p. 28: " La force en commission tant intérieure qu'extérieure, est une sorte de contribution que la nation doit pour le maintien de son établissement public. C'est l'argent & la force individuelle de chaque citoyen qui fournissent l'impôt & l'armée."

[5] *Ibid.*, pp. 9, 28-30; *Préliminaire de la constitution*, pp. 12, note 1, 31-32.

[6] *Vide infra*, chap. vi.

[7] Brougham, Henry, Lord, *Works*, vol. v, pp. 98-99; Beaulieu, C. F., *Essais historiques sur les causes et les effets de la révolution de France*, vol. i, p. 307. He remarks that Sieyes had furnished Mirabeau with the idea of the latter's demand for the formation of a bourgeois guard, early July, 1789.

His views on the religious establishment connect directly with his central thought of building up and intensifying the oneness of France.

A sceptic from his early years, and always scornful of religious dogma,[8] he formally declared to the National Convention that he knew " no other worship than that of liberty and equality, no other religion than the love of humanity and of one's country," and he renounced the income that he received as indemnity from his former benefices, as an " offering to la patrie." [9]

Such an attitude made it easy for him to take the stand that he did take in regard to the Catholic church. He wished to see it completely subjected to the state. Two aspects of his theory, as he developed it during 1789-1790, stand out clearly.

First, the independent position of the French church in relation to the Papacy, which was stated as axiomatic in his *Project for a Constitution* (12 Aug. 1789), and in his *Project for a Provisional Decree Concerning the Clergy* (March, 1790). In these proposals he asserted that the French nation should be completely independent of all supervision, tributes, laws, or pacts, unless, in the future, it should give

[8] *Vide supra*, chap. i, p. 6; chap. v, p. 74, note; *Notice*, pp. 10-18; *Moniteur*, vol. ix, no. 51, Nat'l Convention, session 10 Nov., 1793: " J'ai déposé depuis un grand nombre d'années tout caractère ecclésiastique et qu'à cet égard ma profession de foi soit ancienne et bien connue . . . nul homme sur la terre ne peut dire avoir été trompé par moi; plusieurs m'ont du d'avoir ouvert les yeux à la vérité." Jacob Dupont, when he proclaimed himself an atheist to the Convention (14 Dec., 1792), pictured the French philosophers as teaching their crowds of disciples in the Pantheon, like the ancient Greeks. Among them would be one, he said, " Perfectionnant le système social, montrant dans l'arrêté du 17 juin, 1789, le germe de l'insurrection du 14 juillet . . . ," etc., etc.

[9] *Moniteur*, vol. ix, no. 51, National Convention, session 10 Nov., 1793; *Arch. Parl.*, série i, vol. 78, pp. 716-717. A wave of such renunciations swept over the Convention in this and the preceding session.

its consent to them; that the Gallican church should have control of the public worship voluntarily adopted by the French people (with the proviso that no one should be persecuted for the practise of any other cult); that every ecclesiastic should obtain the sanction of his municipality and district, and that no one ordained by a foreign bishop, or outside of France, or without the aforesaid sanction, should function in the kingdom; and that the National Assembly, with the advice of its ecclesiastical committee, should be given the power to regulate the conditions of eligibility and the mode of election of the bishops, curés and vicars of France.[10]   Such provisions would, of course, have put an end to all control by Rome.   They would have made the French church a purely national affair.

Second, his conception of the accepted religious establishment as an organisation under the control of the government deserves some attention.   While he was fighting for the redemption of the tithe, in August, 1789, he expressly asserted that the church was a public institution, deriving its right to existence from the fact that it served the people; that the clergy was one of those political groups (corps politiques) which, taken together, formed the government; and that the clergy, like the other public powers, was at the beck and call of the national will, and was subject to suppression or reconstitution as the people might direct.[11]   Sometime after the passage of the decree (2 November, 1789) alienating the goods of the clergy, a move in which Sieyes took no part, as might have been surmised from his stand on the redemption of the tithe and its result, he elaborated his conception of the relation of church and state in a lengthy plan dealing with the whole ecclesiastical organisation.

[10] *Arch. Parl.*, série i, vol. viii, p. 424; *Projet d'un décret provisoire sur le clergé, passim.*

[11] " Observations sur les biens ecclésiastiques," in the *Procès-Verbal de l'Assemblée Nationale*, vol. iii, pp. 1-3.

This scheme looked forward to the time when procedure under the constitution should have obliterated the First Estate as an Order and a great corporation, leaving only local ministers of worship. According to its provisions, the Catholic clergy, consisting of bishops, curés and vicars, were to be salaried by the nation. The amount of this salary, the number of the clergy and the manner of their election were all to be decreed by the national legislature. This body should also have complete control of the religious houses, with power to regulate their continuation, modification or suppression and to relieve all novices of their vows. In all cases, the vow of celibacy was to be suppressed, and the priests were to be allowed a special garb only for the performance of the religious office.[12]

This project was rejected by the National Assembly, but it shows Sieyes' interest in establishing state control over the religion accepted by the people as a whole. Moreover, it represented in very real fashion the spirit of the Revolution, for its underlying principles were those of Mirabeau, Alexandre de Lameth, Thouret, Camus and others who were instrumental in putting through the confiscation of church property and the civil constitution of the clergy.[13]

[12] *Projet d'un décret provisoire sur le clergé*, pp. 6, 24-35. See especially, part ii, arts. 6-8, 16-17, 19, 20-21, and part iii, arts. 36, 44. Part ii, art. 19 reads: " Tout privilège exclusif de costume pour un ecclésiastique hors des fonctions de son état est aboli. L'habit d'un fonctionnaire public, quel qu'il soit, ne lui est nécessaire que pour son service. Hors de là, il n'y a que des Citoyens & ce seroit affecter un orgueil trop ridicule chez un peuple libre, que de porter dans la société la prétention de se distinguer des autres par un habit exclusif."

[13] Mirabeau held that religion was a public function, dependent upon the state, and the priest a public functionary who should be taught that his interests were those of la patrie (an unpublished *ms.*, quoted by Robinet, *op. cit.*, vol. ii, pp. 8-10). Lameth argued that the nation was supreme over all "political bodies," among which he classed the clergy (*Point du jour*, vol. ii, p. 74, National Assembly, session 8 August, 1789). Thouret argued along the same lines (*ibid.*, vol. iv, p. 17, National

His failure in pushing these direct plans for national unity through the Assembly is relieved by the success of his greatest step in that direction, the territorial reorganisation of France. We turn now to the reasons which underlay that project.

The chaotic political conditions existing prior to the Revolution cried aloud for improvement. The limits of the kingdom, especially on the eastern frontier, were vague,[14] and the conflicting territorial and political claims of the internal divisions, the pays d'élection, pays d'état, dioceses, généralités, bailliages, etc., formed a hodge-podge that was bewildering in its complexity.[15] Furthermore, a distinctly separatist feeling prevailed in some quarters. The sovereign duchy of Bouillon owned allegiance solely to the king; village after village in Alsace and Lorraine held to the Empire quite as much as to France; Provence was alive with separatism, many of its inhabitants considering themselves a " nation "; Navarre was linked to France by the slenderest of ties; many cities claimed partial independence.[16] Calonne had drawn up for the king's perusal a vivid picture of this confusion which made France a discordant country that it was impossible to govern well.[17]

Assembly, session 30 Oct., 1789). Robespierre asserted that the church only existed for the welfare of the people, and that the people's representatives should control it. He was bitterly against its subjection to outside influence (*Arch. Parl.*, vol. xvi, p. 3, Nat'l. Assembly, session 31 May, 1790). Camus, the leading spirit in putting through the civil constitution of the clergy, was explicit in his assertion that the state could and should control the church (*Arch. Parl.*, vol. xvi, pp. 4-5, Nat'l. Assembly, session 31 May, 1790). These instances might be multiplied.

14 Brette, A., *Les Limites et les divisions territoriales de France en 1789*, p. 3.

15 *Ibid.*, pp. 2, 60, 83 *et seq.*, 97, 109 *et seq.*

16 *Ibid.*, pp. 10 *et seq.*, 33 *et seq.*, 54.

17 " La France est un royaume composé de pays d'état, de pays d'admin-

On the night of 4 August the National Assembly suppressed all local privileges, thus clearing away the principal obstacle to reform, and the following month the Committee on the Constitution drew up a plan of political and territorial reorganisation which, in its main outlines, was adopted by the Assembly. In this manner the multitudinous old divisions were swept away, being replaced by a simple and unified system of départements, districts and cantons.

We have already discussed Sieyes' influence on that Committee and the prominent part that he took in pushing this measure.[18] His zeal was due to his desire to eliminate local differences and prejudices and to develop a unified and compact French nation.[19] "I know of no better means," he wrote, "to make all parts of France into a unit, and all the peoples that divide it into a single nation,"[20] and this ideal was insisted upon throughout the summer and fall of the Revolution's first year. It formed the basis of his constitutional plans in July, plans which he prefaced by urging that all France be brought under the same laws and administra-

---

istration mixtes, dont les provinces sont étrangères les unes aux autres, où les barrières multipliées dans l'intérieur séparent et divisent les sujets d'un même souverain, où certaines contrées sont affranchies totalement des charges dont les autres supportent tout le poids, où la classe la plus riche est la moins contribuante, où les privilèges rompent toute équilibre, où il n'est possible d'avoir ni règle constante ni voeu commun; c'est nécessairement un royaume très imparfait, très rempli d'abus, et tel qu'il est impossible de le bien gouverner " (Quoted by Brette, *op. cit.*, p. 59).

[18] *Vide supra*, chap. iii, pp. 35-37.

[19] *Délibérations à prendre*, p. 40. "Il seroit bien essentiel de faire une nouvelle division territoriale . . . Ce n'est qu'en effaçant les limites des Provinces, qu'on parviendra à détruire tous ces privilèges locaux, utilement réclamés lorsque nous étions sans Constitution & qui continueront à être défendus par les Provinces, même lorsqu'ils ne presenteront plus que des obstacles à l'établissement de l'unité sociale." Cf. the *Aperçu d'une nouvelle organisation de la justice et de la police en France* (s. l., Mars, 1790), art. 86.

[20] *Délibérations*, p. 41.

tion, so that the communes, far from being confederated states, would be integral and essential parts of the same whole.   Unity was dragged into his speech against the royal veto, for he ended by demanding a commission that would draw up a new plan of municipalities and provinces, to prevent the kingdom's dividing itself into a multitude of little republican states and to enable France to form a single whole under a common government.   This same idea underlay the constitutional committee's report, 29 September.[21]

In his pamphlet explaining this report, Sieyes advanced his arguments in a final appeal.   Now or never was the time to make this change, he said.

If we let this opportunity go by, it will not come again, and the provinces will keep perpetually their esprit de corps, their privileges, pretensions and jealousies.   France will never reach that political coördination which is so necessary to make it one great people, governed by the same laws and under the same forms of administration.

There was no ground, he said, sarcastically, for the fear that the provinces would be cut to bits.   No village would be transported from Brittany to Maine, no house torn down, no mountain cut in two; people could go to the same markets as before and maintain the same social and commercial relations.

Once more, calm yourselves, ' But will I cease to be Breton or Provencal? ' ' No, you will always be a Breton, always a Provençal; but you will soon, with us, congratulate yourself on acquiring the status of citizen; we shall all bear, one day, the name of Frenchman, and we shall be able to glorify ourselves

---

[21] *Quelques idées de constitution,* pp. 1 *et seq.; Dire sur le veto royal,* pp. 7 *et seq.;* Thouret's report for the Committee on the Constitution, in the *Procès-Verbal de l'Assemblée Nationale,* vol. v, pp. 5-6, 17.

because of this in places other than the theater, when that name shall designate a free man." [22]

In this project Sieyes did not stand alone. The Committee had the same general purpose; [23] Rabaud St. Etienne's pamphlets advanced the same arguments, and the other plans of territorial reorganisation had the same basis. [24]

Contemporaries avowed that, by 1790, the kingdom of France had become a " patrie," and, in this départemental reorganisation, Sieyes represented the great and patriotic movement working toward that end. " He acted," says a competent authority, " as though France were a moral person, with a life and interests of her own, greater than the lives and interests of the individuals who at a given point in time composed French society." [25]

[22] *Observations sur le nouvelle organisation de France*, pp. 1-2, 12-14. As the preceding passages have shown, Sieyes had an ardent and patriotic devotion to France. His rather frigid temperament did not readily lend itself to the expression of such feelings, but they occasionally broke out. One of the best instances occurs in his speech at the time of his installation as Director, in 1799. He began by asserting the duty of every citizen to respond " lorsque la patrie appelle ses enfans à la servir dans des momens difficiles," and then continued: " En arrivant en France, en touchant le bienheureux sol de la république, mon coeur a tressailli, mes yeux se sont remplis des plus douces larmes. O! mes compatriotes, vous ne connaissez pas la jouissance la plus vive que puisse eprouver un français, si vous n'êtes pas rentrés au sein de votre patrie, après une longue absence " (*Moniteur*, 26 Prairial, VII—14 June, 1799). There is about this outburst a rather touching sincerity.

[23] *Point du jour*, vol. iv, p. 51, National Assembly, session 4 Nov., 1789: " M. Desmeuniers a rétabli les principes qui avoient dirigé le plan du comité; il a cherché, disoit-il, à détruire l'esprit provinciale, pour y substituer l'esprit public, & d'engager tous les Français à concourir à l'administration & à la représentation nationale." *Cf.* Thouret's speeches in defense of the plan (*Procès-Verbal de l'Assemblée Nationale*, vols. v, vi).

[24] *Ibid.*, vols. v, xi, for the plans of Mirabeau, De Bengy de Puyvalle and Rabaud St. Etienne. *Cf.* the latter's *Réflexions sur la division nouvelle du royaume*.

[25] Clapham, J. H., *The Abbé Sieyes*, p. 34.

Sieyes was concerned with yet other projects than these practical steps toward the unification of France. He thoroughly believed in stimulating a feeling of devotion to *la patrie*. Public officials, he asserted, should regard their positions not as rights, but as solemn duties, and the citizens who constituted French society should look upon the state as a most beneficent organisation, which would be only partially recompensed for its services by men's contributions to its welfare.[26] Several methods of inspiring such loyalty were advocated by him.

His *Project for a Constitution* (12 August, 1789) had three distinct provisions of this nature. A " Registry of Honor " was to be established in all the provinces, and upon it the names of the most valuable members of the community were to be duly inscribed as " very worthy or very illustrious citizens; " one day every month was to be set apart to celebrate great national events, and the memory of the nation's illustrious men; there was to be established an annual national holiday to celebrate the promulgation of the constitution, and on that day interest would be stimulated by awards to those

---

[26] *Préliminaire de la constitution*, p. 40: " C'est une grande erreur de prendre l'exercice d'une pouvoir public pour un droit, c'est un devoir. Les Officiers de la Nation n'ont audessus des autres Citoyens que des devoirs de plus; & qu'on ne s'y trompe pas, nous sommes loin, en prononçant cette vérité, de vouloir déprécier le caractère d'homme public. C'est l'idée d'un grand devoir à remplir, & par conséquent d'une grande utilité pour les autres, qui fait naître & justifie les égards & le respect que nous portons aux hommes en place."

Ibid., pp. 24-25: " La société n'affoiblit point, ne réduit pas les moyens particuliers que chaque individu apporte à l'association pour son utilité privée; au contraire elle les aggrandit; elle les multiplie par un plus grand développement des facultés morales & physiques; elle les augmente encore par le concours inestimable des travaux & des secours publics; de sorte que, si le Citoyen paye ensuite une contribution à la chose publique, ce n'est qu'une sorte de restitution; c'est la plus légère partie du profit & des avantages qu'il en reçoit; c'est une mise en commun, dont tous retirent le plus fort intérêt."

parents whose children were distinguished " by their talents and good manners." [27]

The *Project* of which these schemes were a part was not discussed by the Assembly, but a similar idea of his, the establishment of festivals, or " days of rejoicing," whereat the names of young men who had achieved their majority and were adjudged worthy of citizenship should be inscribed on " civic tablets," was taken up by Mirabeau and put through the National Assembly.[28]

Like plans again found expression in his projected national primary school system, which was drawn up during June of 1793 when Sieyes was on the Committee of Public Instruction.

In his writings of 1789, Sieyes had visioned the establishment of national education under the auspices of the state, with a program of instruction covering morals, history, the principles of legislation, elementary national rights, and the national laws. He thought that part of the clergy's wealth might be used in financing such a system. His prominence in connection with the whole idea was such that, in the same year, Mirabeau suggested him to the Court as a suitable minister of education.[29] In 1791, he had written to Clermont-

---

[27] " Projet de constitution," in *Arch. Parl.*, vol. viii, pp. 426-427.

[28] Sieyes, *Observations sur la nouvelle organisation de France*, pp. 23-25. His purpose, he avowed, was to foster emulation, and " c'est surtout dans l'ordre politique que le tableau des Eligibles me semble un des moyens publics les plus utiles."

Mirabeau acknowledged that it was Sieyes' idea, and then went on to stress the need for showing " la jeunesse les rapports qu'elle soutient avec la patrie. La patrie, en revêtant d'un caractère de solennité l'adoption de ses enfans, imprime plus profondément dans leur coeur, le prix de ses bienfaits et la force de leurs obligations." His motion was adopted by acclamation (*Moniteur*, vol. i, no. 79, National Assembly, session 28 Oct., 1789). Cf. Dumont, *Souvenirs*, p. 199, and Duquesnoy, *Journal*, p. 495.

[29] *Vues sur les moyens*, p. 121; *Délibérations*, p. 56; *Quelques idées de constitution*, p. 21; *Projet d'un décret provisoire sur le clergé*, pp. 8, 24-25; Bacourt, *Mirabeau et LaMarck*, vol. i, p. 412.

Tonnerre that education was necessarily a part of the political order, and that the nation was very wise in its desire to eliminate ecclesiastical control of the poor and of education.[30] But he took no part in drawing up a general project until the opportunity presented itself in 1793.[31]

According to this scheme, the national schools, one to every thousand inhabitants, were to provide for the children of France the "education necessary to French citizens." They were to be controlled by a central commission under the immediate authority of the national legislature, which commission should work out a uniform method of regulation and of instruction. The latter should embrace "the intellectual, the physical, the moral, and the industrial aspects of life," and on special days the teachers were to give public lectures on "morality, the social order, rural economy, etc." Each school was to be organised, so far as possible, in replica of the nation's political order. Special attention was to be given to military exercises for the boys, under the guidance of officers of the national guard, and special national officers were to watch over the health of the children. The pupils were to be present at, and have a leading part in, the national fêtes of the cantons and communes, and at one of the cantonal fêtes, that of youth, prizes would be distributed for good conduct, progress, etc. Furthermore, national aid would be forthcoming for the most promising students, and a great national library should be established, and national public libraries opened in every district.[32]

[30] *Moniteur*, vol. vi, no. 291, Sieyes to Clermont-Tonnerre, 13 Oct., 1791.

[31] I follow the copy published in the *Moniteur*, vol. viii, no. 187. This is dated as of the National Convention, session 26 June, 1793, but is really the revised edition that appeared 1 July (*cf.* Guillaume, *Procès-Verbaux du comité d'instruction publique*, vol. i, pp. 507 *et seq.* The changes in the plan will be noted where they are significant.

[32] Arts. i-ii, xvii-xx, xxii-xxiii, xxvii-xxviii, xxxiv, xxxviii, xxxvi-xxxvi, xxxix, xliv.

The plan provided in some detail for national fêtes. These were to be held in the cantons, districts, départements, and in the capital, and were to glorify the seasons, the social order (société humaine) and the French Revolution. The cantons were to celebrate youth, marriage, maternity, the rights of man, the first meeting of the primary assemblies, the sovereignty of the people, etc., nine in all; the district fêtes would take notice of the return of verdure, equality, liberty, justice, etc., also nine in number; the départements would celebrate the seasons, poetry, letters, and the " fête of the destruction of the Orders and the recognition of the unity of the people on 17 June," . . . eight in all. Those to be held at the capital were : on the first day of the year, " the fraternity of mankind; " on 14 July, " the French Revolution; " on 10 August, " the abolition of royalty and the establishment of the Republic; " and, on the anniversary of the proclamation of the constitution, " the festival of the French people." The expenses of these fêtes were to be borne by the nation at large, and prizes were to be given for the best.

Finally, in every canton at least one national theatre was to be established, where the people were to be instructed in music and dancing . . . " that all might coöperate in giving to the national fêtes the utmost beauty and solemnity," thus making possible the presentation of pageants that would recall the most important epochs of history and of the French Revolution.[33]

Sieyes defended the plan vigorously in the *Journal of Social Instruction,* which was published during June of '93 by himself, Condorcet and Duhamel.[34]

[33] Arts. liii-lx, lxi-lxx. The fêtes, according to Danou, a member of the Committee, were the special and personal work of Sieyes. (*Essai sur l'instruction,* quoted by Guillaume, *op. cit.,* vol. i, p. xlix, note i).

[34] The prospectus (drawn up in the epigrammatic style of Sieyes) for

Without doubt, it is time [he wrote] to provide for one of the most essential and most neglected needs of the Republic; let us hasten to reestablish education, but on a plan more natural, more national, more compatible with equality, truth, and usefulness, more worthy, in a word, of our future destinies,

and he went on to urge that men of all ages should be allowed to share in the benefits of this new system, not forgetting to laud the fêtes as stimulating men's social nature and desire for esteem and glory. He accepted a diminution in the number of these celebrations with some difficulty, but remarked that, after all, the main thing was to get them started. They would be a great aid in maintaining what he was pleased to call " the great national family." He waxed eloquent over his vision of 24,000 national schools with nearly 50,000 teachers and 3,600,000 children, " an immense and entirely national establishment " under unitary regulation, using the same text-books and providing a system of uniform instruction.[35]

The fate of this measure has already been described.[36] It was rejected by the Convention, and Sieyes was dropped from the Committee on Education. But it clearly shows his zeal for inspiring the masses with a sense of loyalty to France. In fact, it dwelt far more on stimulating such devotion that it did on the machinery of the system. This was to be worked out in the Bureau of Education.

the *Journal d'instruction sociale* (*Moniteur*, 23 May, 1793) stated that it would be a weekly, purposing to give " l'instruction scientifique dans la politique et faire connaitre à tous quelles sont les ressources nationales dans la population, dans les productions du sol qu'ils inhabitent, dans les contributions, dans les arts et le commerce."

[35] *Journal d'instruction sociale*, no. 3, 22 June, 1793, pp. 82-83, 85-86, 145-146, 152, 156. He had originally planned forty fêtes. The number was reduced by the Committee to thirty, one of those dropped being the " festival of the animal companions of man," a title that evidently excited the hilarity of the Convention.

[36] *Vide supra*, chap. iv, p. 51.

Nor was Sieyes alone in his advocacy of such measures. The Constitution of 1791 had specified that

" there shall be created and organized a system of public instruction common to all citizens. . . . Commemorative days shall be designated for the purpose of preserving the memory of the French Revolution, of developing the spirit of fraternity among all citizens and of attaching them to the constitution, the country, and its laws." [37]

Talleyrand, Danou, Condorcet, and Lanthenas had already drawn up plans for an educational system, and the first two especially showed a similar zeal for inspiring devotion to and love for France. In his famous " Report on Education," Talleyrand stated that the fundamental reason for primary instruction was to teach children those essentials that would make them good citizens, and make them happy. The schools were, to him, agencies for the promotion of national culture, and he laid great emphasis on the teaching of French language and literature. All should be instructed in the principles of the constitution, and, to establish a means of defending it, military drill should form a part of public instruction. He also urged the distribution of prizes, and a system of national fêtes " where the love of la patrie, roused to the heights of enthusiasm, would be made ready to perform prodigies." [38] Danou had asserted that national education should exist " for virtue and for la patrie," and had

[37] *Moniteur*, 16 Sept., 1791.

[38] *Procès-Verbal de l'Assemblée Nationale*, vol. lxx, " Rapport sur l'instruction publique fait, au nom du Comité de Constitution, par M. Talleyrand-Perigord." See especially pp. 11, 15, 106 *et seq.* His project, he said (p. 77), was to form an " institution vraiment nationale, soit parce qu'ils seront déterminés & coordonées conformément au voeu de la Nation, soit surtout parce qu'il n'en est aucun qui ne tende directement au véritable but d'une Nation libre . . . : mais c'est particulièrement dans les moyens qui vont être mis en activité, que ce caractère national doit plus fortement s'exprimer."

provided: that the principles of the French constitution should be studied in the primary schools of the system which he envisaged; that the most elementary classes should learn to read from a book containing expositions of morality drawn from history, and also containing the bases of the French constitution; that a uniform system of military instruction should be established under the direction of an officer of the national guard; and that in the upper schools there should be read weekly a journal containing a résumé of world political affairs, and of the activities of the French National Assembly.   In the spring of 1793, Lanthenas had published a project which, by its very title, included instruction in morals and the nature of public opinion, and in the use of national fêtes, together with the " means of linking these to the national government." [39]   Sieyes, in his plan of education, was following the general tendency when he sought to use the schools in developing loyalty to *la patrie*.

It is obvious that Sieyes considered France a distinct entity, potentially able to will and to act as such, and that he held the French to be a people with particular characteristics distinguishing them from other European peoples.   His mind was fertile with projects for creating a unifying self-consciousness among this special people.   He advocated political democracy and the abolition of privilege; he opposed decentralizing tendencies, such as the growth of powerful municipalities, and federalism; he urged universal military training and control of religion and education by the state, and sponsored projects for stimulating devotion to the French state; and he put through the territorial reorganisation with the avowed aim of ending particularism and of furthering unity.

These various activities were not the chance experiments

[39] Danou, C.-P.-F., *Plan d'éducation présenté à l'Assemblée Nationale*, pp. 2-3, 9, 11; Guillaume, *op. cit.*, vol. i, p. 379.

of a well-meaning humanitarian. They were not born of a vague desire to do something for the benefit of the world in general. On the contrary, they are concrete evidences of a political philosophy that was held by a very shrewd and able man. Sieyes loved France. He wanted to see his country prosperous and powerful. Because of this, he sought an objective that would command the enthusiastic loyalty of all Frenchmen. He found this rallying-point in his concept of France as a nation, and by his activities and plans he tried to awaken in his fellow-citizens a consciousness of their country's worth, to center their interests and affections around the altar of *la patrie*. That is why he stands out as one of the nationalist leaders of the French Revolution.

CHAPTER VII

NATIONALISM. FOREIGN POLICY

THE year 1795 marks a change in the activities of Sieyes. During the earlier part of the Revolution, he, in common with many others who had ideas akin to his, had preached the general doctrines of national unity and internal nationalism, doctrines which were certainly triumphant. Beginning with the Thermidorian reaction, he interested himself chiefly in diplomacy, and from then until his election to the Directory, in the spring of 1799, his attention was mainly centered upon the foreign policy of his country.

From the viewpoint of nationalist tendencies, this represents an interesting development. Heretofore, he had been concerned with stimulating the national consciousness of France. He now turns to making France the most powerful state in Europe, the dictator of the continent. This intention was not primarily the result of a desire to interfere in other peoples' concerns. What nationalist would ever admit such a motivation? He wanted to give France a dominant position in Europe, because that seemed to him the only way of ending European interference in French affairs. This objective became so important to him that he was willing to brush aside any concepts of justice and fair dealing that might come in his way. France, right or wrong, was his first consideration.

The breaking up of the First Coalition against France began in the winter of 1794-1795. Frederick William II of Prussia, no longer aided by subsidies from England and fearful of losing, through Austro-Russian intrigues, his share in the third partition of Poland, had decided in the fall of 1794 to withdraw his troops from the Left Bank of the Rhine and to open peace negotiations with France. In January, 1795, Barthélemy, the French representative, met the Prussian, Goltz, at Basle, and, 5 April, a treaty of peace was signed which left France in possession of the Left Bank, pending a general pacification of the Empire.[1] Meanwhile, England and Austria had been fruitlessly wrangling over the respective efforts that they should make to reconquer Belgium from France, and Spain was making overtures for peace after defeats which had expelled the invaders from French soil and sent the troops of the Convention pouring over the Pyrenees.

Holland, too, was involved in the general debacle. By November of '94 that country was defenseless. Austria was powerless to cover it, the Prussians had left, and the conduct of the English army was so scandalous that the Dutch longed to be delivered from its tyranny.[2] The French, under Pichegru, advanced with great rapidity, and the stadtholder fled to England. On 25 January, the submission of Holland was announced and the revolutionary, francophile committees seized control of the government. They looked to France for aid and guidance, and immediately began to take steps toward an alliance, as between two equal and independent republics.[3] Such was the state of affairs at the beginning of March, 1795.

The Committee of Public Safety, which controlled the diplomacy of the Republic during this period, was composed

---

[1] Martens, *Recueil des traités,* vol. vi, pp. 495-503; Sorel, *L'Europe et la révolution française,* vol. iv, pp. 132 *et seq.,* 193-195, 228-229; Bourgeois, *Manuel historique de politique étrangère,* vol. ii, p. 122.

[2] Sorel, *op. cit.,* vol. iv, pp. 162-163.

[3] *Arch. des Aff. Etran.,* Corr. Pol., Hollande 586, fols. 91-92. Blauw and Van Dam to the Committee of Public Safety, 1 Pluviôse, III (20 Jan., 1795).

principally of lawyers and regicides.   Forced to play continually for support among the various factions of the Convention, anxious to see firmly established the republic to which its members were irrevocably committed, this body adopted a policy of war and glory to which it consistently adhered.[4] " The Republic," said Merlin de Thionville, " must dictate laws to Europe," and again, " our principle must be that the wolves devour one another . . ., for myself, I believe that peace should be made at the expense of all our enemies, but especially at the expense of the most feeble.   It is by them that we arrive at the strongest."[5]   The " strongest " were England and Austria, and the policy of the Committee in regard to them is well summed up in the words of Dubois de Crancé as " war to the death."   The lesser states of Europe were regarded as pawns to be sacrificed at will in the interest of France.[6]   Such was the spirit, such were the plans of the Committee of Public Safety in the year 1795.

Sieyes came into the Committee on 5 March and went immediately to the diplomatic section, where he concerned himself with the affairs of Holland.   Meyer and Blauw, the Dutch envoys, arrived shortly afterward, and on 13 March drew up for the Committee a paper that asked recognition of independence and stressed the urgency of discussing an equitable offensive and defensive alliance.[7]

[4] Sorel, *op. cit.*, vol. iv, pp. 167-169, 216.   Bourgeois, *op. cit.*, vol. ii, pp. 126, 134.

[5] Reynaud, J., *Merlin de Thionville*, vol. ii, pp. 119-120.

[6] Iung, *Dubois-Crancé*, vol. ii, pp. 179-181 ; Sorel, *op. cit.*, vol. iv, p. 247, and " Les Frontières constitutionelles 1795," in the *Revue Historique*, vol. xix, pp. 55-59.

[7] *Arch. des Aff. Etran.*, Hollande, 586, fol. 222 (20 Ventôse, III—10 March, 1795) ; fol. 245 (23 Ventôse, III—13 March, 1795), " Réflexions provisoires pour les citoyens Sieyes et autres commissaires du Comité du Salut Public nommés pour entrer en conférence avec les ministères plenipotentiaires Bataves ; lesquelles réflexions exigeront des nouveau développements."

The next day, Sieyes drafted a plan that was to form the basis for further negotiations. According to this, Holland was to surrender a considerable amount of territory including the important port of Flushing, pay an indemnity to France of 100 million florins, and make a loan of an equal amount at three per cent. Then, and not until then, the independence of Batavia would be recognized and a treaty of alliance concluded. He further proposed to send an envoy to Holland, with instructions to seize control of what France regarded as her due.[8]

All through this period, as the records show, his was the guiding hand in formulating French policy toward the weak neighbor. French interests must be safeguarded, he wrote to the representatives on mission in Holland, and, until the Dutch agreed to the plan that he had outlined, recognition of their independence must be deferred. France must control such territory as would enable it to dominate the Scheldt and Belgium, to the end that it might " oppose the Scheldt to the Thames, Antwerp to London, and our navy, with its base at Flushing, to the English tyranny over the waters of northern Germany and the Baltic. Such are our political views because such is the great interest of the French Republic." [9]

[8] *Ibid.*, fol. 252, " Plan de négociations " (24 Ventôse, III—14 March, 1795) ; and the note inserted between pp. 451 and 453 in the same volume. This plan had been stated in all its main principles by Merlin of Douai, in a letter to the French representatives in Holland. On 16 Ventôse-6 March, Merlin put his ideas in the form of a treaty and handed this over to Sieyes. This plan is in the Archives des Affaires Etrangères. It has marginal notes in Sieyes' hand-writing. They show his agreement with the idea of French acquisition of Flushing, his willingness to seize all the mouths of the Rhine, if the Convention so decides, and at least one island at its mouth in order to ensure free navigation. As to confiscation of the property of French émigrés in Holland and of that of the " hostile government," which Merlin had remarked should be facilitated by the Dutch, Sieyes notes that " ce n'est pas à eux à rien *ceder,* c'est à nous à *prendre* " (Ibid., fols. 178, 213).

[9] Aulard, *Actes du Comité de Salut Public,* vol. xxi, pp. 286-288 (4

In vain did Meyer and Blauw protest against this high-handed action. The former wrote to Sieyes:

. . . It is with the most grievous indignation that we have learned of your desire to add to the French Republic a part of our territory, of which, according to your own principles, the Batavian Republic should not dispose without the freely expressed consent of the inhabitants of that part of the Republic, and of which, certainly, the French Republic has no need, either for its safety or for its grandeur.[10]

But the French diplomat was adamant. He even increased his demands to include reciprocal freedom of navigation of all branches of the Scheldt, Meuse and Rhine down to the sea, the right to occupy any places the French saw fit to hold, Holland to furnish ships for the campaign, and all Dutch forces to be under the command of French generals. " The Scheldt, Antwerp, and Flushing," wrote Sieyes to the representatives on mission at the Hague, " will do more harm to England than twenty battles in which we are victorious." At the same time, he instructed them to act firmly, by force if necessary, in order to prevent the Hollanders from arming, and to push the States General to a prompt ratification of the treaty.[11]

The Dutch were helpless before this display of arbitrary power. They obtained a statement of the French demands, and Blauw took it to Holland. There the cession of territory excited great indignation and was refused. Blauw returned with a substitute treaty, minus the cession and with

Germ. III—24 March, 1795), and pp. 304-307 (5 Germ., III—25 March, 1795). These letters were sent as representing the views of the Committee of Public Safety.

[10] *Arch des Aff. Etran.,* Hollande, 586, fol. 288, citoyen Meyer au citoyen Sieyes Paris, 6 Germ., III—26 March, 1795.

[11] *Ibid.,* fols. 289, 294, 295, 296; and Hollande, 587, fols., 6, 44-48, 57; Aulard, *Actes du Comité de Salut Public,* vol. xxi, pp. 516-518. This correspondence extends throughout Germ., III—March, April, 1795.

the amount of the indemnity unspecified.[12]   Needless to say, it received scant consideration.   On 2 May, Sieyes wrote to Richard, the representative on mission at Utrecht with the Army of the North, that the Committee had definitely decided, if its treaty was not signed in twenty-four hours, to treat the United Provinces as conquered territory and to make a direct levy on the cities and villages in order to raise the indemnity. The threat was not made good, but a new ultimatum, embodying the previous conditions, was drawn up, and Sieyes and Reubell were sent to Holland in order to force through the final negotiations.[13]

The two commissions arrived at the Hague on 8 May and conferences began immediately, with Sieyes taking the leading part for the French delegation.[14]   On 16 May the treaty was signed.

It put Holland under French control, making it a tool to be used in the war against England.   The Batavian Republic was recognized as " a power free and independent," but this was about all the consideration that it obtained.   An offensive and defensive alliance was concluded for the duration of the war, with provision for its automatic renewal

[12] *Ibid.,* fols. 2, 6, 8, 9, 13, 43, 73, 85, 86 (12 Germ.-7 Flor., III, 1-26 April, 1795).   Fol. 79 (6 Flor., III—25 April, 1795) is Merlin's brutal note to the Dutch envoys as to delay in presenting the Dutch answer, " oui ou non."

[13] *Ibid.,* fols. 93, 97 (13, 15 Flor., III—2, 4 May, 1795) ; for the pointment of Sieyes and Reubell, see Aulard, *Actes du Comité de Salut Public,* vol. xxii, p. 617, National Convention, session 14 Flor., III—3 May, 1795.

[14] *Arch. des Aff. Etran.,* Hollande, 587, fol. 113, Sieyes and Reubell to the Committee of Public Safety, 21 Flor., III—10 May, 1795.   The letter was in Sieyes' handwriting.   " Vous pouvez être bien persuadés," he wrote, " que nous marcherons sur la ligne de l'intérêt de notre patrie..." See also fol. 122, Blauw and Meyer to the Committee of Public Safety, 24 Flor., III—13 May, 1795; and fol. 153, Reubell to the Committee of Public Safety, Amsterdam, 3 Prairial, III—22 May, 1795.   ". . . Sieyes, qui a eu tout le poids de la besogne pénible et difficile. . . ."

whenever either country found itself at war with England; neither was to treat for peace with England without the consent of the other; Holland agreed to maintain a French army of occupation (25,000 men), and to furnish heavy naval and army contingents, which, when acting with the French, should submit to the orders of the French commanders; all Dutch Flanders west of the Scheldt was ceded to France, thus giving that country access to Antwerp; Flushing was put permanently under French control; all principal rivers were opened to French navigation; and France was to receive an indemnity of 100 million florins for expenses incurred in freeing the Dutch from their oppressors.[15]

You obtain, [said Sieyes to the Convention,] you obtain new military and naval strength in one of the most important parts of the globe, in the seas of Germany and of the North. The Thames should see with anxiety the future destinies of the Scheldt. Thus the French Republic, which, merely by the strength of its position, should play in the south a great rôle in the Mediterranean, and which can, in the ocean on the west, oppose great forces to English tyranny, acquires in the north the only thing which it lacked, a grand and superb naval and commercial future.[16]

The Convention ratified the treaty amid scenes of the greatest enthusiasm. On Sieyes' motion, the Conventionnels received the Dutch ministers plenipotentiary, gave them the fraternal kiss, and ordered that the flag of the United Provinces be hung with that of the French Republic in the hall of the Convention.[17] Possible twinges of conscience

[15] Martens, *op. cit.,* vol. vi, pp. 532 *et seq.; Arch. des Aff. Etran.,* Hollande 587, fols. 135-136.

[16] *Moniteur,* vol. xii, no. 249, Nat'l. Convention, session 2 Prairial, III—21 May, 1795.

[17] *Ibid.,* vol. xii, nos. 252, 277, Nat'l. Convention, sessions 8 Prairial, 4 Mess., III—27 May, 22 June, 1795.

found no open expression, for equity plays little part where national interests are at stake. Two months later, the policy of France was aptly summed up by Sieyes in a dispute over the indemnity. " How is it, citizen," said one of the Dutch envoys, " that you, who made the declaration of the rights of man, are going to dispoil and maltreat us so harshly? " The reply, as might be expected, was epigrammatic: " Principles are for the schools, interest is for the state." [18]

Sieyes manifested this same spirit in negotiations with Spain that took place in the autumn of 1795. Manoeuverings for peace had been going on while he was busy with Dutch affairs. They were concluded by Barthélemy and Yriarte at Basle, 22 July, 1795, the principal provision being that the Spanish part of San Domingo was ceded to France. Almost immediately the Committee of Public Safety instructed Barthélemy to push for a commercial agreement coupled with an offensive-defensive alliance, and Sieyes took charge of the ensuing diplomatic proceedings.[19]

He had already manifested a keen interest in Spanish affairs. While the peace discussions were under way, he had suggested to the government that the treaty should include a consignment of Spanish sheep and horses to be selected by French agents, and, 15 April, he had drawn up a treaty project by which Spain would have ceded thirteen ships of the line, Guipuscoa, and New Orleans, as well as San Domingo.[20]

[18] Bailleu, *op. cit.*, Gervinus to Hardenberg, 18 Aug., 1795.

[19] *Arch. des Aff. Etran.*, Mém. et docu., France, 653, Colchen, commissioner of Foreign Affairs, to Barthélemy, Paris, 1 Fruc., III—18 Aug., 1795; Martens, *op. cit.*, vol. vi, pp. 542 *et seq.;* Barthélemy, *Papiers,* vol. vi, pp. 81 *et seq.*

[20] *Arch des Aff. Etran.*, Corr. Pol., Espagne, suppl., vol. 25, fol. 22; *Arch. Nat'l.*, AF iii, 63, dossiers 2, 6. Sieyes signed some of the instructions sent to Barthélemy during the latter part of May, but his name soon disappears from the documents.

In August he wrote to the army of the Pyrenees, expressing his keen satisfaction over the treaty concluded at Basle.[21]

As soon as he was put in charge of the negotiations, he manifested his desire to make Spain subject to the will of France. The joint treaties of commerce and alliance which Sieyes urged in the name of the Committee [22] were sweeping in their scope. The commercial treaty was to provide for certain reciprocal restorations of properties and business favors, and at the same time give the French a position of special privilege in Spain. All French business men who had been expelled were to be reinstated with full indemnity. All were to have most-favored-nation privileges, and, under the auspices of their consuls, were to form a " Corps de nation," with the right to appeal to the French authorities in their disputes with the Spanish government and the privilege of meeting together in order to consult their special interests. They should be subject to trial only in military courts, thus being put entirely outside the civil jurisdiction of Spain, and must be regarded as French unless they had formally renounced their allegiance to their native land.[23]

To this was to be joined the following offensive and defensive treaty of alliance, which, as France was then at war with England, was designed to draw Spain into the war as a

---

[21] *Arch. des Aff. Etran.*, Espagne, 637, fol. 126, letters of Sieyes to Meillan and to General Servan, Paris, 24 Therm., III—11 Aug., 1795.

[22] *Ibid.*, Mém. et docu., Espagne, 210, fol. 20, Sieyes and Boissy to Barthélemy, 29 Ther., III—16 Aug., 1795; and Corr. Pol., Espagne, suppl., vol. 25, the Committee of Public Safety to Barthélemy, 29 Therm., 4 Fruc., III—16, 21 Aug., 1795. In all communications with Barthélemy in regard to Spain, Sieyes takes the lead. Where several members of the Committee sign, his name is always the first, and despatches were often signed by him alone.

[23] *Arch. Nat'l.*, AF III, 61, dossier 9. " Minute de Sieyes." This contained the articles of the proposed commercial treaty sent to Barthélemy 4 Fruc., III—21 Aug., 1795. There were no reciprocal provisions for the favors asked.

French satellite. Both agreed to aid one another against all enemies. The power furnishing succor should contribute a heavy naval contingent within three months, and at least 18,000 cavalry and a proportional train of artillery. The Power asking aid should be allowed to send commissioners who would satisfy themselves that the aid would be forthcoming. There must be no discussion of the need, the succors must be completely under the control of the nation demanding them, and their expense must be entirely borne by their own country. Peace should be negotiated only in common.[24] The objective, of course, was the crushing of England. Portugal's accession was expected and then the negotiations would have " closed to our common enemy all European ports from Gibraltar to the Texel." [25]

Yriarte was disposed to favor an alliance, but resented the commercial treaty as an infringement of Spanish rights, and in this Barthélemy agreed with him. But Sieyes was obdurate, and insisted that they must be joined together.[26] The situation was further complicated by the ill-health of Yriarte,

[24] *Arch. Nat'l.*, AF III, 61, dossier 9, " Minute de Sieyes," 5 Fruc., III —22 Aug., 1795; Barthélemy, *Papiers,* vol. vi, pp. 115-119.

[25] *Arch. Nat'l.*, AF III, 61, dossier 9, Committee of Public Safety to Barthélemy, 10 Fruc., III—27 Aug., 1795. The Texel is an island off the coast of Holland, north of the Zuyder Zee.
Sieyes also urged the necessity of freeing Italy from the Emperor's dominance, and bringing that country into a league with France and Spain that should eliminate English control of the Mediterranean (*Ibid.,* Sieyes to Barthélemy, 18 Fruc., III—4 Sept., 1795; *Arch. des Aff. Etran., Espagne,* corr. pol., suppl., vol. 25, fol. 113, Committee of Public Safety to Barthélemy, 3 jour comp., III—19 Sept., 1795). All these projects, of course, foreshadowed Napoleon's Continental System.

[26] *Arch. Nat'l.*, AF III, 61, dossier 9, Barthélemy to the Committee of Public Safety, 16 Fruc., III—2 Sept., 1795; dossier 10, same to same, 5 Vendém., IV—27 Sept., 1795; dossier 9, Sieyes to Barthélemy, 18, 26, 28 Fruc., III—4, 12, 14 Sept., 1795; *Arch. des Aff. Etran.* Mém. et docu., France, 284, fol. 28, " Précis de la situation," 30 Brum., IV—21 Nov., 1795.

who died in December of 1795, and the negotiations languished, despite Sieyes' desire for immediate Spanish participation in the war.   In vain did he invoke the wrath of the French people if Spain continued to be dilatory.   It was not with a coldly calculating ministry, but with the leaders of a free people that Spain had to deal, he told Barthélemy, and the French nation, its sentiments deeply involved where Spain was concerned, would be permanently alienated from that country if this favorable moment for reaching an accord should be neglected.   In vain the resentful Committee of Public Safety wrote that Yriarte's objections were " wounding to the national dignity of France." [27]   Nothing was accomplished under the Convention, and it was only a year later, when Sieyes' influence on diplomacy had long since lapsed, that the alliance was concluded.[28]   But the tenor of these negotiations shows his zeal for securing what he considered to be the national interests of the French people.

He not only sought French dominance over weaker nations.   His plans included the extension of French territory to the Rhine, and the political redivision of central Europe in such a way that France would be the supreme master of the Continent.

While he was on the Committee of Public Safety, he drew up a plan of general pacification that was astonishing in its scope.[29]   It begins with a series of dogmatic assertions.   A

[27] *Arch. Nat'l.*, AF III, 61, dossier 10, Sieyes to Barthélemy, 4 Vendém., IV—26 Sept., 1795; *Arch. des Aff. Etran.*, corr. pol., Espagne, suppl., vol. 25, fol. 122, 8 Vendém., IV—30 Sept, 1795.

[28] Martens, *op. cit.*, vol. vi, pp. 656 *et seq.* This treaty contained, in general, the same provisions as to aid, and stated that Spain would compel Portugal to close her ports to the English.   There was no commercial treaty at this time.

[29] *Arch. des Aff. Etran.*, mém. et docu., Allemagne, 117, fol. 29, copie. " Projet de traité de paix présenté au Comité de Salut Public par l'organe du Citoyen Sieyes membre du dit comité en l'an III de la République." No date.

lasting peace is necessary; to obtain this, France must extend its territory to the Rhine, and must never depart from the principle that the Rhine is its eastern boundary; the great German powers must be removed from the Right Bank, and replaced by smaller states that will look to France for support; the Germanic constitution must be preserved because it is useful to France, but the ecclesiastical states, too susceptible to control by Austria and Prussia, must be suppressed; these steps must be taken boldly, because the safety of France is involved.

Then comes a series of twenty-nine articles for the carrying out of this plan. France is to get the Left Bank, and the navigation of the Rhine is to be made free. All central Europe is overturned. The Empire remains, but the ecclesiastical states are wiped out and their lands distributed among their neighbors. Prussia and Austria gain heavily, but in such a way that they are thrust to the East. Between them and the Rhine looms up a new constellation of states, Bavaria being the most prominent, all of which have gained territory by this French proposal, and all of which will supposedly be properly grateful to their benefactor.[30]

He held firmly to this plan, and especially to the Rhine frontier, during the remainder of his stay on the Committee of Public Safety. Just before his return from Holland, that body had weakened on the Rhine barrier and had instructed Barthélemy, at Basle, to aim principally at acquiring the Low Countries.[31] Sieyes' disappointment was great and,

---

[30] Reubell had similar ideas, and Dentzel, one of the representatives on mission, had sent a similar plan to the Committee of Public Safety on 20 Pluv., III—8 Feb., 1795 (*Arch. des Aff. Etran.*, mém. et docu., France, 652, fols. 13, 14. *Cf.* Guyot, *op. cit*, p. 120). Certainly, Napoleon's Confederation of the Rhine comes to mind.

[31] *Arch. des Aff. Etran.*, Prusse, suppl. 10, fol. 205, Committee of Public Safety to Barthélemy, 3 Prairial, III—22 May, 1795; *Cf.* Barthélemy, *Papiers*, vol. v, pp. 283-284.

as soon as he reached Paris, he drew up a minute stating that he " could not look without groaning at the map of this fine country between the Meuse and the Rhine, which, being neither Dutch nor French, would remain a theater of war," and urged his firm belief that the negotiators could get this land, and so end the affair " for the greatest good of France and of Europe.[32]

In June, the Committee, strengthened by military victories, returned to the policy of conquest, and, 15 June, he acted as its spokesman in a long conversation with Gervinus, the Prussian envoy. They met at the Tuileries, in a room so dimly lighted that they could hardly distinguish one another, and there Sieyes laid down the law in the interests of France. This country desired peace, he told Gervinus, but it must be a " glorious peace," one that would, at the same time, give Germany a stable system by strengthening some states and weakening others. After this preliminary, which was obviously based on his *Projet de traité,* he urged the necessity of Prussia's making " useful alliances." The Prussian suggested that French influence in Germany would be greatly increased by not retaining any conquered land, whereupon Sieyes rose in wrath, demanding that Gervinus show his plan of pacification, if he had one. Prussia, Sieyes asserted, was taking too much to heart the question of the Left Bank, and the interests of the Germanic states which meant nothing to her. " He is very difficult as to character," wrote Gervinus, sadly, " hard, cutting, shrewd, full of a philosophic pride, and so enamoured of his opinions that he can scarcely suffer the slightest contradiction, having, besides, his head full of his Platonic and Aristotelian republics; he and his party see them everywhere." [33]

[32] *Arch. des Aff. Etran.,* Hollande, 587, fol. 158, p. 268, "minute de Sieyes", Paris, 6 Prairial, III—25 May, 1795.

[33] Ranke, *op. cit.,* vol. v, pp. 94 *et seq.,* Gervinus to Hardenberg, 15

Two weeks later, Sieyes wrote to Merlin de Thionville in the same strain. France needed peace, he said, but the only way to get it was to " show ourselves strong, march forward, and inspire terror among the cabinets that make war on us." To go back to the old frontiers would be a bad mistake, a show of cowardice before vindictive enemies. The doughty Merlin answered that he was in absolute agreement with these sentiments.[34]

On 3 July, Sieyes and two other strong partisans of the Rhine frontier left the Committee, and that body once more looked favorably upon the old limits, but the party of conquest and republics kept on working in the Convention.[35] A month later, Sieyes and Reubell came back to the Committee, and the extension of frontiers was once again the order of the day. Thereafter, the policy of the Committee swayed back and forth in response to internal events and the fortunes of war,[36] but Sieyes remained constant in devotion to his plan, as is shown by the attitude of the Prussian court and the remarks of his erstwhile colleague, Reubell.[37] Two

June, 1795; Bailleu, *op. cit.*, vol. i, pp. 398, 407, Gervinus to Hardenberg, 15 June, 21 July, 1795. Treilhard and Merlin de Douai were present at this meeting, but Sieyes acted as spokesman. Gervinus remarked that Sieyes would yet establish a new republic on the lower Rhine.

[34] Reynaud, *Merlin de Thionville*, vol. ii, p. 221, Sieyes to Merlin, 10 Mess., III—28 June, 1795, and Merlin to Sieyes, 16 Mess., III—4 July, 1795.

[35] Aulard, *Actes du Comité de Salut Public*, vol. 25, pp. 192-194, Gillet, ex-membre du Comité de Salut Public, à Merlin (de Thionville), Paris, 18 Mess., III—6 July, 1795; Bailleu, *op. cit.*, vol. i, p. 407, Gervinus to Hardenberg 21 July, 1795. Gervinus listed Sieyes, Louvet and Chénier as the leaders of this party. They were called the Brissotins, because Brissot had advocated these republics.

[36] Sorel, " Le Comité de Salut Public et la question de la rive gauche du Rhin," and " Les Frontières constitutionnelles, 1795," in the *Revue Historique*, vol. 18, pp. 298 *et seq.*, and vol. 19, pp. 22 *et seq.*

[37] Bailleu, *op. cit.*, vol. i, p. 29, instructions to Sandoz-Rollin, Prussian ambassador to France, 21 Oct., 1795; *Arch. Nat'l.*, AF III, 81, Reubell

years later, Mallet du Pan wrote to Vienna, " Reubell, Merlin and Sieyes direct French foreign policy almost without contradiction and on the same original plan. They want to parcel out all Europe, piece by piece." [38]

Men were always prone to overestimate the significance of the ex-abbé's silences, and there is no evidence to show that he was actively interesting himself in diplomacy at the time when Mallet made this observation. But that his general views remained the same throughout this period is highly probable. In 1798, when he was called upon to take the position of French envoy extraordinary at Berlin, he attempted to carry out the general policy that he had adopted four years earlier.

An alliance with Prussia had been the dream of French statesmen since 1794,[39] and Caillard, at Berlin, had made the

to the Committee of Public Safety, 2 Fruc., III—19 Aug., 1795; and AF III, 68, mémoire, 22 Mess., IV—10 July, 1796.

[38] Mallet du Pan, *Correspondance inédite . . . avec la cour de Vienne,* vol. ii, p. 361, letter dated 16 Nov., 1797.

In December, 1795, Sieyes proposed, undoubtedly for the Directory, to Boccardi, minister of the Republic of Genoa, that France help the Republic gain territory around the Gulf of Spezia, and, in return, that Genoa cede to France San Remo and two other cities. Nothing came of it, but, says Guyot, " all the Directory's political program in connection with Genoa was in this conversation." It certainly illustrates Sieyes' expansionist ambitions. *Cf.* Guyot, *op. cit.,* p. 143, and Colucci, G., *La Repubblica di Genova e la Rivoluzione Francese,* vol. ii, pp. 319-320, Boccardi to the Genoese Senate, 2 Dec., 1795.

[39] Dubois de Crancé had proposed in 1794 an alliance with Prussia, Spain and Sardinia, in order to crush Austria and England (Sorel, *L'Europe et la rév. franç.,* vol. iv, pp. 221-222). The Directory (Dec., 1795) ordered Caillard, at Berlin, to seek such an alliance. " Ces instructions de Caillard," says Guyot (*op. cit.,* pp. 127-128), sont importantes, car les projets d'alliance prussienne sont l'un des points de la politique directoriale qui ont le moins varié, et les efforts pour faire adopter ce programme n'ont pour ainsi dire pas cessé jusqu'à la fin du regime. C'était la clef de voûte du systeme. . . ."

Three times, from 1796 to 1798, the alliance had been offered by France, and had been refused (*vide supra,* chap. iv).

last unsuccessful attempt in May of 1798.[40] He was immediately succeeded by Sieyes, whose choice by Talleyrand was agreeable to the Directory.[41]

The instructions drawn up for the new minister directed him to keep Prussia at least neutral, but to strive for an offensive-defensive alliance, and clearly showed the Directory's hope of a wider alliance with Spain, the Helvetian, Batavian and Italian Republics, Denmark and Sweden, and most of the secondary states of the Empire.[42]

The alliance was doomed to failure. Surrounded by spies from the beginning, faced by the hostility of the court and the Fabian policy of a conservative Prussian ministry, which even refused a conference to harmonize weights and measures on the ground that it was dangerous to tamper with a single one of the " fundamental principles " of the Prussian state,[43] Sieyes struggled in vain to obtain a close rapprochement.

But this was not his only line of procedure. The ex-abbé was much interested in formulating plans for the pacification of Europe, plans that would establish the dominance of his own country over all others. He was a firm believer in close connections with the smaller German states, and he had hardly had time to gain a thorough knowledge of the situation at Berlin when he began sending reports as to these weaker members of the Empire.

[40] Bailleu, *op. cit.,* vol. i, pp. 469-471. Caillard to the Min. of For. Aff., 5, 22, 29 May, 1798.

[41] *Ibid.,* vol. i, pp. 191 *et seq.* Sandoz-Rollin from Paris, 9 May, 1798; *Arch. Nat'l.,* AF III (3358), note of Talleyrand, 18 Flor., VI—8 May, 1798; *Dropmore Papers,* vol. iv, p. 272. Report of Mme. de Rochechourart to Grenville, July, 1798.

[42] *Arch. des Aff. Etran.,* Prusse, 223, fol. 61, Paris, 4 Prairial, VI—23 May, 1798. There is another copy in the "mém. et docu.," Prusse, 9, fol. 5.

[43] *Arch. des Aff. Etran.,* Prusse, 223, fol. 137, Prussian ministry to Sieyes, 16 Aug., 1798.

They were, he held, necessary to France as protégées and allies, and must be supported. With their assistance, the Republic would control the western coasts of Germany and be able to exclude the English from all the markets and ports between Gibraltar and Holstein, or even the North Cape. There must never be established on the banks of the North Sea, he wrote, any great military power " capable of escaping from our protection and allying some day with Great Britain." The mouths of the Elbe and Weser must be controlled by weak but devoted allies, thus cutting communications between England and Prussia, and a similar ally must be established on the right bank of the Rhine. At the proper time the Directory must take a hand in shaping conditions " so favorable to French prosperity and the repose of Europe." Talleyrand replied that these principles were his, and that he was making every effort to shape the government's policy in this direction,[44] but even this did not satisfy the man at Berlin. All the estates of the Empire, he wrote, must be linked to France. " Heretofore you seem to have intended giving them to Prussia: take them for yourself." He advised sending agents to stir them up, especially Hesse-Cassel which had " just grievances " against Prussia. Eventually two unions of these states, north and south, would be formed. Then Prussia, her position seriously weakened, would be forced to rely upon the friendship of the Republic. The Directory was in accord with this project, and tried to rouse the Landgrave of Hesse-Cassel against

[44] *Arch. des Aff. Etran.*, Prusse, 223, fols. 105, 116, Sieyes to Talleyrand, 26 Mess., 6 Ther., VI—14, 24 July, 1798; Bailleu, *op. cit.*, vol. i, p. 482, note, Talleyrand to Sieyes, 6 Aug. 1798; Pallain, *op. cit.*, p. 354, Talleyrand to Sieyes, 6 Aug., 1798, ". . . Votre principe est le mien, je l'ai toujours professé. Reculer l'Autriche parce qu'elle est ennemie et qu'elle doit longtemps l'être; recular la Prusse, parce qu'elle est amie et qu'elle le deviendra davantage si sa puissance reçoit les modifications dont elle est susceptible."

Prussia. It offered him an alliance, only to suffer a rather ignominious failure.[45]

Sieyes continued to insist upon the necessity of such combinations. The old Germanic constitution, he wrote, was certain to fall to pieces and the great, hereditary powers would profit, " if the still more powerful will of the Executive Directory neglects to define with a republican sagacity the true character of the great epoch in which we live." [46]

A letter to Talleyrand, in January of 1799, really epitomizes his diplomatic efforts of this period:

It seems inevitable to me, Citizen Minister, that the European political system will, within a short time, experience considerable changes. The various governments will, more or less promptly, obey that natural inclination which inspires those who are in distress to lie in the easiest possible positions, and you will see each one finish by gently placing itself in its own center of gravitation. The French Republic is not far from its true equilibrium. Give it, in Italy, a not too feeble ally, one powerful enough to serve as a useful auxiliary, and it will be at peace on the continent. At the same time, have the hardihood to establish in north-western Germany from the Yssel or the Ems as far as the Baltic, a league or confederation as completely representative in form as possible, and then wage against Great Britain a war in which her fleets would be impotent, and you will have peace upon the sea, a veritable peace, effective and permanent for you and for all western Europe. Your representatives in foreign countries will then be able to show themselves Republicans without fear of injuring diplomatic negotiations, and, to speak the truth, the Republic will be recognized politically, morally and civilly.

[45] *Ibid.,* Prusse, 224, fol. 178, Sieyes to Talleyrand, 8 Fruc., VI—25 Aug., 1798; Prusse 225, fols. 145, 187, Sieyes to Talleyrand, Berlin, 21 Nivôse, 17 Pluv., 8 Ventôse, VII—10 Jan., 5, 26 Feb., 1799; Bailleu, *op. cit.,* vol. i, pp. 485-486, note, Talleyrand to Rivals, 26 Sept., 1798.

[46] *Arch. des Aff. Etran.,* Prusse, 223, fol. 211, Sieyes to Talleyrand, 25 Fruc., VI—11 Sept., 1798.

In other words, the true character of the epoch was to be its French character. The only real pacification, Sieyes held, would be one obtained and enforced by his own country. He was utterly unable to see any other solution of Europe's problems. To him, Haugwitz was utterly perfidious in attempting to persuade the secondary states that they were threatened by the ambition of their neighbor across the Rhine, and that they should cleave to Prussia rather than to France.[47]

He himself took steps to promote a feeling of trust and confidence in France among those states, urging upon them the necessity of " quitting the antechambers of Berlin and Vienna." France, he believed, should pose as the protector of Bavaria, and the French foreign minister ordered Alquier, at Munich, to make every effort with the Elector toward forming a South German League under French protection.[48] At the same time, a stream of letters urging a North German League under French control as necessary to peace, the ruin of England and the establishment of " a good political and commercial influence in the north," finally drew from Talley-

[47] *Arch. des Aff. Etran.,* Prusse 224, fol. 17.   Sieyes to Talleyrand, 11 Vendém., VII—2 Oct., 1798.

[48] *Ibid.,* Prusse, 224, fol. 22, Sieyes to Talleyrand, 18 Vendém., VII— 9 Oct., 1798; Prusse, 225, same to same, 1 Ventôse, VII—19 Feb., 1799; Bailleu, *op. cit.,* vol. i, pp. 498-499, Talleyrand to Alquier, 17 March, 1799, and Talleyrand to Sieyes, 19 March, 1799.   In this last letter, writing of the Bavarian project, Talleyrand said: " . . . le Directoire, frappé des mêmes considérations qui vous ont si souvent porté à désirer qu'on plaçât en Allemagne une espèce d'état intermédiaire, s'occupe en ce moment de sa formation."   He was hopeful that the Elector would succumb to the idea.

Jean DeBry, one of the French representatives at Rastadt, had seen the desirability of French domination over the smaller German states, and had advocated the formation of a South German League similar to that proposed by Sieyes (*Arch. des Aff. Etran.,* Allemagne 675, fol. 115. "Essai sur l'intérêt comparé de la république française."   This paper by DeBry is dated 9 Mess., VI—27 June, 1798).

rand the assurance that, as soon as possible, such a plan would be put into action.[49] The conservatism of the central European governments rendered these schemes fruitless. Sieyes himself recognized that the opposition of Prussia to any such northern league would be intransigeant, and by April, 1799, he was convinced that Bavaria and the other southern states had more fear of being revolutionized by France than of being dominated by Austria.[50] But the plans of the French diplomat clearly demonstrate his desire to make France the political dictator of Europe. Nor had he abandoned his dream of the Rhine frontier. The man who would have calmly seized the Hanoverian possessions in order to enforce a general peace,[51] was as zealous in 1799 as he had been in 1795 for extension of territory. His argument was based on the necessity of obtaining peace and the free navigation of the Rhine. Both, he was certain, could only be assured by French control of the Left Bank, and any further discussion of that control could only be an obstacle to peace. He told the Prussian ministry, in a note vigorously upholding the principle of secularization to indemnify the lay princes shorn of their Left Bank possessions, that, if any further discussion arose over the disposition of the Left Bank, it would not be the French Directory that would have to reproach itself with having fruitlessly and unnecessarily retarded the

[49] *Arch. des Aff. Etran.*, Prusse 223, fols, 105, 116, 178, 211; Prusse 224, fols. 144, 170; Bailleu, *op. cit.*, vol i, p. 499. Talleyrand to Sieyes, 19 March, 1799.

[50] *Arch. des Aff. Etran.*, Prusse, 224, fol. 144, Sieyes to Talleyrand, 19 Nivôse, VII—8 Jan., 1799; Prusse, 225, fol. 42, Sieyes to Talleyrand, 17 Germ., VII—6 April, 1799.

[51] *Ibid.*, Prusse, 224, fol. 144, Sieyes to Talleyrand, Berlin, 19 Nivôse, VII—8 Jan., 1799: "Quand je jette les yeux sur le passé, je ne puis m'empêcher de croire que la République pouvoit être depuis longtemps en paix avec Angleterre, et par conséquent avec le continent, si elle avoit mis la main sur les importantes possessions du Roi d'Angleterre en Allemagne. Qui nous en a empêché? La Prusse."

conclusion of peace.[52]   He rejoiced over the fall of the re-
putedly impregnable fortress of Ehrenbreitstein, opposite
Coblentz, as indicative of the determination of France to
guarantee herself by her own might against the enmity of
Europe. "The possession of Ehrenbreitstein and similar
places," he wrote to Talleyrand, "is the best guarantee that
we could have against English or Russian threats. You
authorized me, at a time when it was a question of making
peace by negotiation, to promise in your name that this very
important fortress would be demolished and given up; a
favorable opportunity for making such a declaration has
never presented itself, and I have not done so." [53]   It would
be hard to find a leader of the revolution who demonstrated
more clearly than did Sieyes his belief in the principle, so
dear to many more recent nationalists, that a nation's safety
depends upon strength and the power of arms and forcible
annexations of territory.

It was inevitable that a certain amount of zeal for propa-
gating republicanism should attach to this insistence upon the
preëminence of France.   The man who, in 1795, had " seen
republics everywhere," and especially between France and
Germany, was in 1798, still wedded to the idea of overthrow-
ing the monarchical system whenever possible.[54]   In the
autumn of that year, Talleyrand formulated a plan for ob-

[52] *Ibid.*, Prusse, 224, fol. 73, Sieyes to Talleyrand, 20 Brumaire, VII—
10 Nov., 1798; fol. 116, Sieyes to the Prussian ministry, 30 Frim., VII—
20 Dec., 1798.

[53] *Ibid.*, Prusse, 225, fol. 32, Sieyes to Talleyrand, 3 Germ., VII—23
March, 1799.

[54] Ranke, *op. cit.*, vol. v, pp. 103-104, Gervinus to Hardenberg, 15 June,
1795; Bailleu, *op. cit.*, vol. i, p. 407, Gervinus to Hardenberg, 21 June,
1795.   In this opposition to monarchies, he was in accord with Jean
DeBry, who remarked that the issue was " du système privilégie hérédi-
taire ou système d'égalité représentative " (*Arch. des Aff. Etran.*,
Allemagne, 675, fol. 201, " Observations conjecturales," 20 Brum., VII—
10 Nov., 1798).

taining peace, a plan that envisaged a renunciation of indemnities, save for hereditary princes dispossessed on the Left
Bank, and a guarantee of the status quo in Italy by France,
Prussia, Switzerland and Spain.[55] Sieyes was dissatisfied
with this latter arrangement. " We have been mistaken in
not wiping out all the Italian monarchies," he wrote; [56]
" You seem to me to be putting yourself in opposition to the
natural course of affairs. You are combating there [in
Italy] that force of events which rules in the political order
as the law of gravitation governs the physical order; and I
add that, in saying this, I believe that I am listening to reason
alone. Sentimentality would have a different language." [57]
He spoke to the Prussian ministry about the renunciation of
indemnities, but said nothing about Italy or about guarantees
by Spain and France. Talleyrand's project was stultified,
for Haugwitz believed that Sieyes was trying to trick him
into a hostile step toward Austria.[58]

From time to time, other instances of this republican
fervor manifested themselves. The cherished confederation
of small North German states was to be founded on a basis
"the most representative possible," [59] and in February of '99

[55] Pallain, *op. cit.*, p. 359. Talleyrand to Sieyes, 19 Therm., VI—6
Aug., 1798; *Arch. des Aff. Etran.*, Prusse 223, fol. 209. Talleyrand's
report to the Directory on the Berlin negotiations (23 Fruc., VI—9 Sept.,
1798). This report was approved by the Directory.

[56] *Ibid.*, fol. 187. Private letter of Sieyes to Talleyrand, 12 Fruc.,
VI—29 Aug., 1798.

[57] *Ibid.*, Prusse 224, fol. 5. Sieyes to Talleyrand, Berlin, 4 Vendém.,
VII—25 Sept., 1798. Talleyrand replied that Sieyes was surely mistaken;
that liberty was very feebly rooted in Italy, and that " Nos armées sont
sans cesse en peril au milieu de ceux qui nous doivent leur existence
politique " (*Ibid.*, fol. 24, Talleyrand to Sieyes, 19 Vendém., VII—10
Oct. 1798).

[58] *Geheimer Staatsarchiv*, 1798, ii, fol. 250; 1798, iii, fols. 56, 63.
Memoir of Haugwitz, 24 Sept.; king to Sandoz, 24-25 Sept. Quoted by
Guyot, *op. cit.*, pp. 862-863.

he wrote to Talleyrand that if the Emperor would only embroil himself with Prussia and Russia (by seeking to acquire Bavaria) he would probably abandon Venice and the Italian Tyrol, leaving those countries to be gained to the representative system. During that time there would be " peace and increase of credit in Europe and good business for the Republic, with most happy chances for the ulterior progress of the representative system, commencing with Bavaria itself, and without our having to mix ourselves up in the affair." [60]

Then, in August, when he was such a power on the Directory, came one last evidence of his affection for the French system. At that time, Prussia and Spain offered their mediation in the war, if France would agree to the reëstablishment of the stadtholder in Holland and to the Meuse as a boundary instead of the Rhine. Sieyes replied that to the latter he would agree, but that he would never abandon the Batavian Republic.[61]

[59] *Arch. des Aff. Etran.,* Prusse 224, fol. 170. Sieyes to Talleyrand, 7 Pluv., VII—26 Jan., 1799. A little later, he expressed his belief that republicanism was inevitable in this confederation (*Ibid.,* Prusse 225. Sieyes to Talleyrand, 19 Ventôse, VII—9 March, 1799.

[60] Bailleu, *op. cit.,* vol. i, p. 497. Sieyes to Talleyrand, 19 Feb., 1799.

[61] *Geheimer Staatsarchiv,* Berlin, Rxi, 89, Frankreich, 1799, ii, fols. 240, 241, 252. Sandoz to the king of Prussia, 24 Therm., VII—11 Aug., 1799. The king to Sandoz, 2, 9 Fruc., VII—19, 26 Aug., 1799. Quoted by Guyot, *op. cit.,* p. 902. Guyot remarks: " Ainsi, jusqu'au dernier moment, les deux programmes furent en presence: la propagande d'un côté, avec la gloire de fonder des Etats ; de l'autre, la frontière du Rhin, le vieux programme herité de la monarchie par le Comité de l'an III. Comme Bonaparte à Leoben, Sieyes choisit la propagande." Many factors, however, must have contributed to this choice. The stadtholder, for instance, would have been inimical to France and French interests, and Holland was an essential ally in the struggle with England. But it cannot be doubted that Sieyes' zeal for republicanism played a part in that decision. He had written to Talleyrand, in March of '99, that, for the monarchical states, " Initium sapientiae timor Republicae." (*Arch. des Aff. Etran.,* Prusse 225, fol. 19, Berlin, 22 Fruc., VII—12 March, 1799).

What is the meaning of the above illustrations from Sieyes' diplomatic career? What do they signify? That he wanted to establish peace in Europe? Yes. That he wanted to see the republican system triumph as against the monarchical? Yes. But, more than this, they show that he meant to establish these things by means of, and for the sake of, a colossal France that would bestride the Continent, overturning and creating states, and forcing its will upon the rest of the world. That was the inner significance of Sieyes' foreign policy. He was not an imperialist, as has been shown he was not interested in acquiring territory beyond the natural frontiers. He desired the peace and prosperity of Europe, but, first of all, he proposed to establish the peace, prosperity and predominance of France. " Those who have accused me of being a friend of Austria have lied," he told Sandoz in 1795, " those who have represented me as a friend of the Prussians have also lied; I am a Frenchman and nothing else." [52] We can do no better than to take him at his own valuation.

[52] Bailleu, *op. cit.,* vol. i, p. 41. Sandoz-Rollin to the king of Prussia, 28 Dec., 1795.

CHAPTER VIII

The Final Years. An Appreciation

The events of 18-19 Brumaire (9-10 November, 1799) marked the beginning of a new order in France. On the latter date, the Corps Législatif appointed two commissions to revise the constitution, and then proceeded to decree a provisional government, with Bonaparte, Sieyes and Roger-Ducos as " Consuls of the French Republic." These three worthies promptly took an oath of " inviolable fidelity to the sovereignty of the people; to the French Republic, one and indivisible; to equality, liberty and the representative system,"[1] and once again the government began to function.

The new constitution was, naturally enough, the affair of greatest moment, and the commissions immediately concerned themselves with it. Sieyes was supposed to have a plan already drafted and the expectation was general that he would take a leading role,[2] but his star was swiftly sinking. At the first meeting of the Consuls, Ducos had abandoned him for Bonaparte,[3] and the latter, by softening the measures of proscription taken by the ex-abbé against the Jacobins,

---

[1] *Moniteur*, 20, 21, 23 Brum., VIII—11, 12, 14 November, 1799. It is interesting to note that the Parisians took little interest in the coup d'état (Staël-Holstein, *Correspondance*, Brinckman to the Swedish Chancellor, 10 Nov., 1799).

[2] *Publiciste*, 27 Brum., VIII—18 Nov., 1799, quoted by Aulard, *Paris sous le Consulat*, vol. i, p. 12; *Journal des Républiçains*, 29 Brum., VIII—18 Nov., 1799; Boulay, *op. cit.*, pp. 3-4.

[3] Cambacérès, *Eclaircissements*, quoted by Vandal, *op. cit.*, vol. i, p. 409; Las Cases, *Journal*, vol. i, p. 242. Sieyes may well have said, as the memoir writers report, "nous avons un maître" (Napoleon, *Memoirs*, vol. i, pp. 106-107; Rovigo, *Mémoires*, vol. i, pp. 242-243; Bourrienne, *Mémoires*, vol. iv. p. 130).

immediately established for himself a reputation for magnanimity at the expense of his rival.[4] Omens were not favorable to the success of Sieyesian constitutional schemes.

Several of these have come down to us, although none of them directly.[5] Their main outlines were similar. A list of active citizens [6] formed the basis of the proposed political structure. They were to choose one-tenth of their number to form a communal list, eligible for local office. This list reduced itself by one-tenth to form a départemental list, and

[4] Staël-Holstein, *Correspondance*, pp. 352-353, 367-368. Brinkman to the Swedish Chancellor, Paris, 10, 28 Nov., 1799; Fauriel, C., *Les Derniers jours du Consulat* (Paris, 1889), p. 6, and note 2; Jourdan, "Notice sur le 18 brumaire," in *Carnet Historique*, vol. vii, pp. 161-172, Feb., 1901; Cambacérès, *Eclaircissements*, authority used by Vandal, *op. cit.*, vol. i, pp. 425-427.

[5] There is the plan dictated to Boulay de la Meurthe (*Théorie constitutionnelle de Sieyes*, pp. 10-42), the one outlined to Danou and reported by him to Mignet (*Hist. de la rév. franç.*, vol. ii, pp. 264-270), and the one given in the *Moniteur* (10 Frim., VIII—1 Dec., 1799). Vandal (*op. cit.*, vol. i, p. 495) and S. Schnaffner (*Die Sieyes'chen Entwürfe und die Entstehung der Verfassung des jahres VIII*, pp. 2 et seq.) regard the Moniteur plan as the most valuable.

The Danou plan comes under Vandal's fire (*op. cit.*, vol. i, p. 500, note i) as being not of 1799 but of 1795. I agree with Clapham (*op. cit.*, p. 246, note iii) in regarding this as a mistake. It resembles Sieyes' plans of 1799 far more than that of 1795. Clapham (*op. cit.*, p. 242) holds that Boulay's outline is the most authoritative. This seems to me to be correct. The plan as there given was dictated by Sieyes to Boulay (*Théorie constitutionnelle de Sieyes*, p. 4), and Boulay is obviously writing from notes taken at the time. He gives a clearcut and lucid exposition of the Sieyesian ideas.

It appears that Sieyes had no plan in readiness at the time of the coup d'état. "J'ai bien quelques idées dans la tête," he remarked to Boulay (20 Brumaire), "mais rien est écrit, et je n'ai ni le temps ni la patience de les rédiger "(*Ibid.*, pp. 3-4).

[6] Estimated at 6,000,000 in the Boulay plan. Danou gives them as 1/10 of the general population. The *Moniteur* project restricted activity to those paying a direct tax equivalent to at least ten day's labor. There is little about universal suffrage in these estimates, despite Neton's assertion to the contrary (*op. cit.*, pp. 405-406).

a further reduction of one-tenth formed the national list from which the highest officials of the land were to be chosen.[7]

The framework of the national government was to consist of a *Tribunat,* representing popular interests, that was to propose laws and discuss them before a *Jury Législatif* which should not discuss, but should pass or reject the laws proposed. A *Collège des Conservateurs,* renewing itself always from the national list, was to choose the members of the two legislative bodies and protect the constitution by its right of absorption, a curious provision by which it could forcibly elect into its own membership any individual whom it deemed dangerous to the safety of the state. It also elected the titular head of the government. This individual was called the *Grand-Electeur.* He took office for life, but had no power, save as he appointed or dismissed the chief executive heads of the government. If he threatened to become dangerous, the *Collège des Conservateurs* could absorb him.[8]

Such was Sieyes' plan. Its central idea, as is easily seen, was such a division of power as would render forever impossible the danger of despotic control by either legislature or executive.

Rumors about it became prevalent before Sieyes had it ready for presentation, and its author heard that Bonaparte was dissatisfied. The general's opposition was a serious matter, and the theorist, much alarmed for his cherished scheme, thought of seeking the support of the constitutional

[7] Boulay, *op. cit.,* pp. 12-14. The *Moniteur* and Danou plans are based on the same principle.

[8] This is the essence of the plan outlined by Boulay. The other two are in principle the same.

These ideas bear considerable resemblance to those of Spinoza. See Pariset, G., "Sieyes et Spinoza," in the *Revue de synthèse historique,* vol. xii, pp. 309-320, Jan.-June, 1906.

The idea of the *Grand-Electeur* had been advanced by Sieyes in 1789 (*Observations sur la nouvelle organisation de la France,* p. 36).

committees in an endeavor to carry things with a high hand.
Boulay persuaded him to try for a rapprochement with Bonaparte. In this matter, Boulay, Roederer and Talleyrand
acted as go-betweens, and engineered conferences between
the two.

These meetings were far from amicable. Bonaparte ob-
jected to various parts of the plan, especially to the limited
powers of the *Grand-Electeur,* and to the danger of his being
" absorbed." [9]   The story ran about that the general crossed
out offending passages with a stroke of his pen.[10]   " Do you
want to be king, then? " Sieyes asked on one occasion.[11]   He
was exceedingly discontented, and affairs were in a critical
state.   He threatened to withdraw the plan entirely, to appeal
to the people, to exile himself in the country or even leave
France. Bonaparte remained obdurate, despite these dire
menaces.

At this juncture, Boulay, who was president of the Five
Hundred's committee, stepped in with a happy compromise.
The two committees were united and began drafting a constitution on the basis of Sieyes' plan. This was carried on
under the leadership of Danou. Bonaparte then turned toward Sieyes with a friendly gesture, and after that the two
committees and the three consuls met every day in Bonaparte's salon to examine and discuss the new project.[12]

[9] Boulay, *op. cit.,* pp. 44-48; Roederer, *Oeuvres,* vol. iii, p. 303; Gohier,
Mémoires, vol. ii, p. 44; Las Cases, *Journal,* vol. iv, part 2, pp. 145-146.
This unreliable authority gives the story of Napoleon's saying, " Et comment avez-vous pu imaginer, M. Sieyes, qu'un homme de quelque talent
et d'un peu d'honneur voulût se résigner au rôle d'un cochon à l'engraisse
de quelques millions? "

[10] Staël-Holstein, *Correspondance,* p. 371, Brinckman to the Swedish
Chancellor, 2 Dec., 1799; Reinhard, *Lettres,* p. 112, Paris, 18 Nivôse,
VIII—8 Jan., 1800.

[11] *Grouvelle mss.,* quoted by Vandal, *op. cit.,* vol. i, p. 504.

[12] Staël-Holstein, *Correspondance,* pp. 374-376, Brinckman to the
Swedish Chancellor, 6 Dec., 1799; Boulay, *op. cit.,* pp. 48-58; Boulay de
la Meurthe, "*Life,*" pp. 112-115.

These meetings came more and more under the ascendancy of the man who was destined to rule France for the next fifteen years, and the Constitution of the year VIII bears the seal of Bonaparte, rather than of Sieyes or Danou.[13] The lists of eligibles were retained in modified form, the départements and local groupings kept their place, the *Tribunat, Collège des Conservateurs* (changed in title to *Sénat conservateur*) and *Jury Législatif* remained, but the Sieyesian balance of power and responsibility, the central feature of his plan, was replaced by an ominous centralization of control in the hands of the executive. Many local offices were made appointive by the government, instead of being chosen from the communal list by the départemental officials; the *Tribunat,* shorn of its power to propose laws, could only criticize or praise; the *Sénat Conservateur* was deprived of its right of absorption, of the power freely to choose its own members and of its right to censor the *liste nationale;* finally as a crowning stroke, the *Grand-Electeur* and his two Consuls were rejected for an executive consisting of three consuls, the First Consul being vested with significant and far-reaching powers.[14] The government remained republican in name, but in essence it was monarchical.[15]

[13] For Bonaparte's skillful balancing of Sieyes' and Danou's proposals against one another, see Schaffner, *op. cit.,* pp. 31-34, and Vandal, *op. cit.,* vol. i, p. 512.

[14] He promulgated the laws (the " government," which is to say, the First Consul, also proposed them), appointed and dismissed at will the members of the council of state, ambassadors, officers of the army and navy and local administration officials, and named all judges, save the justices of the peace and those of the supreme court (juges de cassation).

In tracing these changes, I have followed the constitution of the year VIII as given in the *Moniteur,* 25 Frim., VIII—16 Dec., 1799.

[15] Staël-Holstein, *Correspondance,* p. 383; Brinckman to the Swedish Chancellor, 16 Dec., 1799.—"Vous verrez, Monsieur, par la charte constitutionnelle même que le gouvernement actuel est effectivement monarchique, quoique sous les formes d'une artistocratie graduelle."

Sieyes could not prevent these changes. In fact, he seems to have offered little opposition to some of them. Pushed into the background by a more vigorous, a greater personality, perhaps deceived by the committees on whom he had hoped to rely, his ill-humor was great and his one thought was to retire.[16] He might, had he so chosen, been one of the subsidiary Consuls, for Bonaparte was agreeable,[17] but Sieyes preferred a less conspicuous post. In company with Roger-Ducos, he became a senator, and these two, together with Cambacérès and Lebrun, chose the majority of the Senate, which then completed itself and proceeded to the election of officers.[18] On Christmas Day, 1799, it elected Sieyes as its first president, an office which he held for three months. It had been rumored that he would be made president for life, and Mme. Reinhard sarcastically observed that the rest would be good for him, and that the new dignity would, perhaps, cure him of his bad humor.[19]

Wealth also came his way, for Bonaparte took the attitude that Sieyes had performed great services to the state and should be rewarded. On 19 December, the First Consul wrote to the Commission of the Five Hundred that Sieyes

[16] Boulay, *Théorie constitutionnelle de Sieyes*, pp. 62-63, 70; *Grouvelle mss.*, quoted by Vandal, *op. cit.*, vol. i, pp. 510, note i, 514; Bailleu, *op. cit.*, vol. i, p. 353, Sandoz-Rollin from Paris, 12 Dec., 1799.

[17] Staël-Holstein, *Correspondance*, p. 384, Brinckman to the Swedish Chancellor, 16 Dec., 1799; Roederer, *Oeuvres*, vol. iii, p. 304; Napoleon, Memoirs, vol. i, p. 151.

[18] *Moniteur*, 4 Nivôse, VIII—25 Dec., 1799; *Arch. Nat'l.*, CC 972, Procès-Verbal du Sénat-Conservateur, session 3 Nivôse, VIII—24 Dec., 1799; Buchez et Roux, *Hist. Parl.*, vol. xxxviii, p. 291, constitution de l'an VIII, art. 24.

Grouvelle (Vandal, *op. cit.*, vol. i, p. 547) asserts that Sieyes dictated the names of the senators first chosen.

[19] *Arch. Nat'l.*, CC 972, Procès-Verbal du Sénat-Conservateur, session 4 Nivôse, VIII—25 Dec., 1799; Reinhard, *Lettres*, pp. 102-103, Paris, 23 Frim., VIII—14 Dec., 1799.

should be given some "outstanding witness of national recognition." Action was immediate, and Sieyes was awarded the national domain of Crosne (an estate lying in the département of the Seine-et-Oise), or its equivalent, as a "national recompense."[20] Difficulties arose in regard to this estate, which was restored by law to its former owner, but in its stead a grant was made of the farm of the Menagerie at Versailles, two houses in Paris and some "national furniture."[21]

There is no positive proof of collusion on the part of the principals in this transaction, but it is tainted with suspicion and is highly discreditable to Sieyes. Public opinion was aroused by his acceptance of these substantial rewards, exactly for what, no one knew, at a time when the government found itself unable to do anything toward alleviating the general distress of the country. It was generally felt that Bonaparte was taking advantage of Sieyes' egotism and cupidity as a means of bribing him into a state of inactivity. Rumor had it that he would indignantly reject the offer of Crosne. "His acceptance, pure and simple, has covered him with a general contempt," wrote Brinckman, and the Prussian ambassador noted a little later, that he had "fallen into a profound oblivion. No one speaks of him and no one regrets him."[22]

[20] *Arch. Nat'l.*, AFIV, 13 A, 28 Frim., VIII—19 Dec., 1799, and ADXVIII, A 63, 30 Frim., VIII—21 Dec., 1799; Aulard, *Registre des délibérations du Consulat Provisoire*, pp. 100-103; *Moniteur*, vol. xxi, no. 91, Five Hundred, session 30 Frim., VIII—21 Dec., 1799.

[21] *Arch. Nat'l.*, AFIV, 57, AFIV, 68, 9 Flor., 7 Prairial, VIII—29 April, 27 May, 1800; Aulard, *Paris sous le Consulat*, vol. i, p. 86, quote from the *Journal des hommes libres*, 20 Nivôse, VIII—10 Jan., 1800.

[22] Staël-Holstein, *Correspondance*, p. 395, Brinckman to the Swedish Chancellor, 30 Dec., 1799; Bailleu, *op. cit.*, vol. i, p. 363, Sandoz-Rollin from Paris, 23 Jan., 1800; Barras, *Mémoires*, vol. iv, pp. 137-138; Pasquier, *Mémoires*, vol. i, p. 147. The *Diplomate* (25 Nivôse, VIII—15 Jan., 1800) spoke satirically of his vanished glory. Consul, Director,

Of course he was numbered among the opposition. Cambacérès seems to have controlled the Senate, but clubs remained, and the expression of opinion. Mme. Récamier's salon, which was hostile to Bonaparte, was frequented by Sieyes. He accused Talleyrand of ingratitude and perfidy in going over to the General.[23] A temporary absence from Paris, early in January, brought out all sorts of rumors as to flight, or even imprisonment in the fortress of Ham, rumors scornfully denied by the *Moniteur,* and set at rest by an apparent rapprochement with Bonaparte.[24] What his political designs were, no one knew. A duel was fought that arose from a dispute as to what they might be. But the police watched him closely.[25]

Then came Marengo, and, on the chance of an Austrian victory, or at least of Bonaparte's death, a plot was organized to overthrow the government. Sieyes was undoubtedly a party to this, although his aims are not clear. He was suspected of wanting to replace the General by Carnot, and another story ran that he was desirous of establishing the Orléanist dynasty, but all plans were wrecked by the victor-

Ambassador, Legislator, all had disappeared, it said. Only the Abbé Sieyes remained.

A quatrain of the time expressed the general feeling:

> " Sieyes à Bonaparte a fait présent du trône,
> Sous un pompeux débris croyant l'ensevelir ;
> Bonaparte à Sieyes a fait présent de Crosne
> Pour le payer et l'avilir."

[23] Vialles, P., *L'Archichancelier Cambacérès*, pp. 205-242; Challamel, *Les Clubs contre-révolutionnaires*, pp. 566-567; Bailleu, *op. cit.*, vol. i, p. 358, Sandoz-Rollin from Paris, 5 Jan., 1800.

[24] Reinhard, *Lettres*, pp. 113-115, Paris, 18 Nivôse, VIII—8 Jan., 1800; *Moniteur*, 22 Nivôse, VIII—12 Jan., 1800; Bailleu, *op. cit.*, vol. i, p. 364, Sandoz-Rollin from Paris, 26 Jan., 1800. The wags of Paris made the most of the occasion with a Latin pun: " Si es, ubi es ? "

[25] Aulard, *Paris sous le Consulat*, vol. i, pp. 264, 272, 282, 326, 331, 335-336.

ious return of the First Consul.[26] Then, for a period of time, he was closely watched, being regarded as one " behind the curtain," directing and stimulating opposition to the government, and one witness, at least, believed that the " purification " of the *Tribunat* in Nivôse, X (Dec.-Jan., 1801-1802), was in part due to a desire to eliminate some of Sieyes' adherents.[27]

But, as Napoleon's star continued to rise, Sieyes apparently resigned himself to the inevitable. Already he had been active in the proscription of the Jacobins that followed the attempted assassination of Napoleon on the famous " Third Nivôse " (24 Dec., 1800), and, in the following spring, the police noted that he was trying to persuade the First Consul of his devotion.[28] So far as can be ascertained, he was not distinguished for his opposition to the Empire. According to Roederer, he was altogether too well satisfied with his own position to be much of an opponent, and, although at first he was against conferring the Imperial dignity, he absented

[26] Girardin, S., *Journal*, vol. ii, pp. 175-182; Iung, *Lucien Bonaparte*, vol. i, pp. 410-413, Lucien to Joseph Bonaparte, 24 June, 1800; Aulard, *Paris sous le Consulat*, vol. i, pp. 442, 445, *et passim*, police reports for June–July, 1800. The police were positive that Sieyes was of the Orléanist faction. *Cf. Dropmore Papers*, vol. vi, p. 291, Edwards to Grenville, 12 Aug., 1800.

It is interesting to note Napoleon's denial, at St. Helena, that Sieyes ever conspired against him (Las Cases, *Journal*, vol. vi, part 2, pp. 139-140).

[27] *Cf.* Girardin, *Journal*, vol. iii, pp. 237, 254-255, and Lanfrey, *History of Napoleon*, vol. ii, p. 206; *Arch. Nat'l.*, F 7,3829, police reports; Aulard, *Paris sous le Consulat*, vol. i, pp. 533, 536, and vol. ii, pp. 12, 38 *et passim*, police reports. These reports continue, with considerable frequency, until 1803. But it at least seems probable, considering his character, that his attitude was more in conformity with his remark to Bailleul: " Laisser faire le Gouvernement, il s'en fera de lui-même." (*Arch. Nat'l.*, F 7,3829, police report 3 Pluv., IX—23 Jan., 1801).

[28] Gohier, *Mémoires*, vol. ii, pp. 117 *et seq.*; Aulard, *Paris sous le Consulat*, vol. ii, p. 238, police report, 5 April, 1801.

himself when the day came for the final vote.[29] At the time when Moreau was brought to trial by Napoleon, for implication in the Cadoudal conspiracy of 1804, Sieyes acted in a manner that was thoroughly discreditable. He could have materially assisted Moreau by testifying to the latter's refusal to take the lead in the coup d'état of 1799, but, when asked to do so, he replied " that he hoped the general would be good enough not to ruin him by insisting upon his request." It is possible that Sieyes was not entirely a disinterested spectator of the intrigues of this period, for the police reported him as a " discreet " partisan of Moreau.[30]

Nor was he averse to accepting honors that came, probably, as a result of his passivity. He was made a member of the political economy section of the Institute, when the old Academy was revived under that name by Napoleon, and, in the same year (1804), he and his brother Joseph were named officers of the newly constituted Legion of Honor. In 1808, all Senators were created hereditary Counts of the Empire, and in May of that year Napoleon conferred the title and granted to " our dear and beloved Sieyes " an elaborate coat of arms with " liveries blue, white and green." [31] It was the crowning glory—or the crowning shame. Thereafter he disappears from view until the fateful days of 1814-1815.

In 1814, when the Empire was fast crumbling under the

[29] *Arch. Nat'l.*, CC, 976, Procès-Verbaux du Sénat Conservateur, *passim*; Roederer, *Oeuvres*, vol. iii, p. 514; Clapham, *op. cit.*, p. 257.

[30] Lanfrey, *op. cit.*, vol. ii, p. 421, mss. notes of the tribune Moreau, communicated to Lanfrey by the Countess de Courval; *cf.* Fauriel, C., *Les Derniers jours du Consulat*, p. 414, and Lafayette, *Mémoires*, vol. v, pp. 213-214; Aulard, *Paris sous le Consulat*, vol. iv, p. 750, police report of 20 Germ., XII—10 April, 1804.

[31] *Arch. Nat'l.*, CC 240, fol. 136; CC 980, Procès-verbaux du Sénat-Conservateur, session 11 March, 1808; AFiv, 6049; Duvivier, P., *L'Exil du Comte Sieyes*, p. 3; Teissier, O., *Les Députés de la Provence*, p. 114. On 3 April, 1813, Sieyes and some fifty others were given the Grand Cross of the Imperial Order of the Reunion.

onslaughts of the Allied armies, his name appears once more in the records. Fearful though he was of the Bourbons' return,[32] he bowed to the inevitable, giving his consent by letter to the senatorial edict decreeing Napoleon's fall, and voting for the constitutional charter of 6 April.[33] During the First Restoration he remained inactive.[34] The beginning of the Hundred Days found him wary and suspicious,[35] but he accepted membership in the Chamber of Peers, and, with Roederer, was elected to a committee which drew up an address of fulsome flattery and devotion to the Emperor.[36] With the news of Waterloo, he showed a last vestige of his old vigor, publicly urging the necessity of fighting to the end.[37] But the tide was too strong. The end had come for both the leaders of Brumaire.

[32] Reinhard, *Lettres*, p. 338, Paris, 17 Feb., 1814, "... Sieyes, qui rédoute avant tout le retour des Bourbons, avait repris courage et s'est montré au cercle."

[33] Buchez et Roux, *op. cit.*, vol. xxxix, pp. 501, 520; Pasquier, *Mémoires,* vol. ii, p. 319.

[34] Neton gives the story, based on various memoirs, of his having refused Fouché's importunities to join in intrigues against the government, but his sources can scarcely be trusted.

[35] Barère, *Mémoires*, vol. iv, p. 434, for an account of a meeting with Sieyes at the Tuileries on 22 March, 1815. The anecdote is sufficiently circumstantial to allow of belief. "... sur quoi peut-on compter avec cet homme qui est sans cesse à se révolutionner lui-même?," remarked Sieyes.

[36] *Arch. Nat'l.*, AF iv, 7067, no. 1, 2 June, 1815, decree naming the members of the Chamber of Peers; CC 988, *Procès-Verbaux du Sénat-Conservateur, Chambre de Pairs*, sessions 3, 5, 11 June, 1815. The address reads in part,—"Vous avez manifesté, Sire, des principaux qui sont ceux de la nation. Ils doivent être les nôtres. Oui, tout pouvoir vient du peuple, est institué pour le peuple; la Monarchie constitutionnelle est nécessaire au peuple françois comme garantie de sa liberté & de son indépendance." It goes on to compliment him on his submission to forms and constitutional rules (obviously a reference to the Acte Additionnel), and promises unswerving adherence in defeat or victory.

[37] Lavalette, *Memoirs*, vol. ii, p. 195; Joseph Bonaparte, *Mémoires,* quoted by Neton, *op. cit.*, p. 443.

It was only natural that the old regicide, who had rallied to the usurper during the Hundred Days, should be among those proscribed by the Bourbons. The storm broke in January, 1816, for the Law of Amnesty, when it was promulgated, specifically excluded the regicides who had supported the " usurper." [38] He fled to Belgium, arriving at Brussels during the latter part of January. This city he selected as his place of residence, and there, during 1817, he purchased, for 19,000 francs, a house in the rue de l'Orangerie, a street then on the outskirts of the city and a few minutes walk from the park. He kept this dwelling with the aid of a household of six servants. His nephew, Jean Sieyes, son of his younger brother Joseph, made his home with him, and, marrying in 1819, reared up a family of five children under the roof of the famous man.[39]

At the beginning of his exile he would still discourse most authoritatively upon political questions, and Lord Brougham, who met him in Brussels at the beginning of 1817, found his opinions on the English political situation characteristically oracular, but absurd and ignorant. His activities, however, later reduced themselves to daily promenades in the park and to the quiet social life which drew the fellow exiles together.[40] Of these last, David seems to have been his closest friend. The famous painter did a portrait of Sieyes in 1817, and it was largely due to the latter's advising him not to sacrifice his " honorable independence " that David refused a flattering

---

[38] *Moniteur*, 14 Jan., 1816. It had been rumored in November that Sieyes had fled to Prussia (*ibid.*, 29 Nov., 1815). On 21 March, 1816, a special ordinance expelled him, together with Cambacérès and Merlin, from the Académie Française.

[39] *L'Oracle*, no. 23, 23 Jan., 1816, and the *Journal de la Belgique*, no. 24, 24 Jan., 1816, quoted by Duvivier, *op. cit.*, pp. 6, 8, 18, 20-22, 28.

[40] Brougham, *Works*, vol. v, pp. 101-102; *Memoirs of a Highland Lady*, quoted by Clapham, *op. cit.*, p. 260.

invitation to Berlin, extended by the King of Prussia.[41]   But
the elderly regicide was also intimate with Merlin of Douai
and Thibaudeau, and, with Cambacérès and Ramel, he helped
establish a fund to aid impoverished French exiles.[42]

David died in 1825, and Sieyes' health, never very good,
was failing.   More and more he lived to himself, going out
seldom.   Pressed to write his memoirs, he replied:

Cui bono?   Our work is great enough to be our commentary;
our deeds will inform those curious to know our thoughts, and
all the information we could give would not suffice to guard,
against our faults, those who, coming after us, will only acquire
our wisdom at the price of the same misfortunes.[43]

His banishment ended with the July Revolution, and in
September, 1830, he returned to Paris,[44] where he lived in
obscurity for six more years.   Some glimmerings of his old
self remained.   Boulay asked him, on one occasion, what he
thought of parliamentary government as practised after
1830, and was told . . . " They talk too much, and don't act
enough." [45]   Reinstated in the Academy, his feeble health
would not permit attendance, and Roederer told Lord
Brougham of a touching scene he had witnessed when a delegation from the learned body had sought to persuade Sieyes
to attend.   The old leader spoke of his uselessness as a member of any association, and, conversing in a strain that
showed all too plainly the effects of age, he finally said, . . .

[41] David, J., *Le Peintre Louis David*, pp. 527-530, 589, 649.

[42] Baudot, *Notes Historiques*, p. 291 ; Duvivier, *op. cit.*, p. 32.

[43] *Notice de M. Fortoul*, quoted by Sainte-Beuve, *op. cit.*, vol. v, p. 214.
Barère (*Mémoires*, vol. iv, pp. 353-354) asserts that Sieyes wrote a
notice for a biography of contemporaries that was to be edited by Wahlen
at Brussels, but I have been unable to find any trace of this manuscript.

[44] *Journal de la Belgique*, no. 260, 17 Sept., 1830, quoted by Duvivier,
op. cit., p. 52.

[45] Boulay de la Meurthe, " *Life*," pp. 388-389.

" In short I am no longer able to speak, . . . nor to hold my tongue." [46]   So he lived until he had reached his eighty-eighth year.

The end came on 20 June, 1836, at his house, number 119, rue de Faubourg-Saint-Honoré.   The obsequies took place two days later.   There were no religious rites at the funeral.[47]

A simple tomb, situated near the winding Avenue des Acacias in Père Lachaise Cemetery, marks his final resting place.   Across the top is the single word " Sieyes," and, on the plaque within, this inscription—" Emanuel Joseph Sieyes, né le 3 Mai, 1748, mort le 20 Juin, 1836."   No other reminder of his past is to be found among the simple furnishings, with one exception.   At the back of the tomb there is the statue of a priest in a white robe, who gazes meditatively at a crucifix lying across his bent left arm.   So the symbol of religion stands guard over the ashes of the man who rejected religion and fought his fight alone.

It is easy enough to find flaws in Sieyes.   He was so certain that his way was the right way, that he often became overbearing and arrogant.   " It is always good to present the true principles," he says complacently in *What is the Third Estate,* and this was a concept of his mission here on earth from which he never wavered.   Dumont found him disagreeably conceited, as did Gouverneur Morris and many others.   He was wont to lash out bitterly at those who ventured to disagree with him, and his remarks were not always confined to criticisms of their arguments.[48]   Nor can one too

[46] Brougham, *Works,* vol. v, p. 103; *cf.* Sainte-Beuve, *op. cit.,* vol. v, p. 214, for a similar anecdote recounted to him by some of those who saw Sieyes in the last years.

[47] *Moniteur,* 22 June, 1836; *Journal de la Belgique,* # s 176, 178, 179, June 24, 26, 27, 1836, quoted by Duvivier, *op. cit.,* pp. 54-55.

[48] *Cf.* Dumont (*Souvenirs,* pp. 62-63, 148), Sieyes' correspondence with

severely condemn his unfortunate tendency to lapse into sulky inactivity whenever his hopes were crossed or his plans thwarted. Mirabeau called him " Mahomet." The epithet is a happy one. He was a typical doctrinaire, and the difficulty of dealing with him was enhanced by his lack of confidence in his fellow men. Brinckman found him so convinced of his own superiority, so certain that he was applying rational principles to the solution of all problems, that he was dictatorial and dogmatic, even in discussing questions of morals and philosophy. Constant, who saw much of him at one time, analyzed him not only as fundamentally cold and and unsympathetic but also as being incapable of concealing that trait of his character.[49]

Wilhelm von Humboldt, who met him in 1798, gives what is perhaps the best single estimate of his character. Speaking of the French philosophers, he remarked that,

Of them all, Sieyes is obviously the most profound. . . . But he has not clarified or coördinated his ideas, and he is too proud and impatient to listen to anything new, much less to accept it. He is among those rare individuals of whom one can say with almost perfect truth that, endowed with outstanding powers of thought, and character, they are yet unsuited to either thought or action, and this only because his whole character is passionate—not that this or that passion actually governs him, but because everything that comes from him bears the stamp of passion, of extraordinary vehemence. . . . but he withdraws into himself with an equal sensitivity as soon as he perceives that his ideas are not completely accepted. When he is in the act of contriving anything of magnitude, he has not the firmness to push it to completion, and the fretfulness that checks

Clermont-Tonnerre and Crillon (*Moniteur*, 25, 29 Oct., 7 Nov., 1791), and Mme. de Staël's estimate of his character (*Considérations sur la rév. franç.*, vol. i, pp. 182-183).

[49] Staël-Holstein, *Correspondance*, Brinckman to the Swedish Chancellor, 13 June, 1799; Aulard, " Sieyes et Talleyrand . . . Constant et Barras," in the *Rév. franç.*, vol. 73 Oct.–Dec., 1920, pp. 298-299.

him in this keeps him also from a quiet and mature discovery
of truth.   His thought also bears every trace of a similar quick
and sensitive vehemence; he is uncommonly witty, not in a light
or pleasant manner, but sharply and bitingly.   He presses into
the depths, but these efforts of his are flashes that suddenly go to
the heart of the matter, rather than slow penetration accompanied by persevering exertion.[50]

With all the criticism that this contains, there is real recognition of Sieyes' intellectual strength, a recognition that was
granted more enthusiastically by able French contemporaries.[51]   He had an uncommon power of logical expression,
as his writings show.   They are compact, orderly, clear-cut,
to an astonishing degree; abounding in vigor of presentation
and intellectual force.   Taken by themselves, his political
schemes, his drafts of constitutions, are admirably worked
out systems, and his main idea—government based on the
representative system—is accepted in principle by most of the
modern states.

Nor is this all.   Though many of his projects were rejected, he left a real mark upon the Revolution.   His presentation of grievances, his enunciation of popular rights,
was clear and cogent.   The influence of his first pamphlets
upon the popular mind can never be accurately measured, but
contemporaries were uanimous in testifying to their great
effect.   The famous *What is the Third Estate* together with
his activity in the assembly of the Third Estate, make him
beyond question the outstanding leader in the portentous
events of June, 1789, when the National Assembly was

[50] Humboldt, Wilhelm von, *Neue Briefe Wilhelm von Humboldts an
Schiller*, pp. 221-222,—Humboldt an Schiller, Paris, 23 June, 1798.
Humboldt remarks that he had many conversations with Sieyes.

[51] Duquesnoy, *Journal*, vol. ii, p. 365; Mirabeau, letters quoted by
Sainte-Beuve (*op. cit.*, vol. v, p. 211) and the *Courrier de Provence*,
vol. i, pp. 3-4; Constant, B., letter quoted by Aulard (*Rév. franç.*, vol.
73, Oct.–Dec., 1920, pp. 298-299).

formed and the Revolution began; his attacks upon privilege —and no writer assailed it more constantly—were vindicated on the night of 4 August, when the foundations of political and economic inequality were swept away; he contributed much to the constitution of 1791 by his writings and by his work on the constitutional committee,[52] and, of what he did on this latter body, the départemental redivision of France stands out as the great monument to his ideals and ambitions.

His star sank swiftly, and, though he was never without a coterie of devoted adherents, his subsequent career was fitful and unmarked by great achievements. One more great opportunity was given him in 1799, when, as the most powerful figure on the Directory, he tried to realize his long-cherished scheme of giving France a stable government and a perfect constitution. But he lacked the sustained driving force of a great leader, and France was not ready to be controlled by a doctrinaire. The sword that Bonaparte cast into the balance outweighed all theory, and Sieyes retired for the last time to the obscurity of disappointed hopes and frustrated ambitions.

What is Sieyes' place in the history of nationality and nationalism? National feeling, ebullitions of patriotism, had been known in Europe before his time. Witness the devotion to England that found expression at the time of the Armada, and the love that "la douce France" at times aroused in the hearts of her sons.[53] But the idea of complete allegi-

---

[52] *Vide supra,* chap. iii, pp. 29-32. Mirabeau told Camille Desmoulins many times that Sieyes and he (Mirabeau) were the fathers of the constitution (*Révolutions de France et de Brabant,* # 72, vol. vi, p. 309). In March, 1790, Lanjuinais, speaking before the National Assembly, referred to " Cet homme sublime et profond, à qui l'on doit la Constitution de la France, M. l'Abbé Sieyes." (*Moniteur,* vol. ii, # 91, Nat'l. Assem., session 31 March, 1790).

[53] Stewart and Desjardins, *French Patriotism in the Nineteenth Century,* pp. vi *et seq.*

ance, supreme loyalty, to one's nationality had its main origins in the eighteenth century. By the end of that century, the principal outlines of three philosophies of nationalism are to be clearly discerned.

In England, an aristocratic-political variety of nationalism manifested itself in the writings of Bolingbroke, Blackstone, the younger Pitt, and Burke. The first, as the forerunner, is, perhaps, the best example. This rationalist politician and philosopher believed that society and government rest upon a contractual basis, and that, in some far distant past, nationalities with national differences had been created by the Deity whom he coldly worshipped. Bolingbroke lauded patriotic service, the love of country, and the promotion of national interests in their broadest sense, as the highest and most fruitful of ideals. But his concept of nationalism was primarily an aristocratic one. The perfect nation should be governed by an hereditary, although patriot, king, and by those chosen few, created by God in every nationality, " who engross almost the whole reason of the species : who are born to instruct, to guide, and to preserve." The " herd of mankind " had only to obey. His ideal, like that of other British thinkers of his time, was a national state, ruled by the king and the intelligent with the support of a national church and of the landed and moneyed interests of the country.[54]

Germany, through the voluminous writings of Johann Gottfried von Herder (1744-1803), contributed a nationalist philosophy that was primarily cultural. Herder was a European pioneer in the stimulation of romantic interest in folk-language and folk-literature, a devotee of national history, and thoroughly convinced of the super-excellence of Germany's cultural heritage which he sought to make

[54] Hayes, C. J. H., " The Philosopher Turned Patriot," in *Essays in Intellectual History*, pp. 189-206. Quotations are from Bolingbroke, *On the Spirit of Patriotism, Works*, vol. iv, pp. 187-189.

known to the German people.   His nationalist philosophy, implicit rather than explicit in his numerous works, contains the following essentials; that, as a result of long centuries of environment, education and traditions, each nation, or people, acquires a folk-character or folk-personality; that this folk-character expresses itself by means of the national language, a national religion, and national literature; and that, from this folk-character, so expressed, arises what is known as culture.   Culture is, therefore, essentially national.

The influence of this man was by no means trivial.   He stimulated German interest in Germanic literature, and encouraged the writing of literary histories of Germany; his demand for a science of history stimulated the founding of the Monumenta Germaniae Historica; he preached and practised educational reform, with stress on the study of the German language; and he contributed to the subsequent German belief that a national religion is preferable to any world religion.   In other words, he preached the right of the German nation to exist, and he was answered by the War of Liberation and the flowering of German nationalism in the nineteenth century.[55]

A third kind of nationalism, far more powerful than the other two in its subsequent effects upon the history of Europe, had its origin primarily in France and particularly in the French Revolution.   This is democratic, political nationalism.

Under the French monarchy, the Divine Right kings were, for centuries, symbols of French unity, frequently receiving the almost religious devotion of their people.   So, in a

[55] Hayes, C. J. H., " Contributions of Herder to the Doctrines of Nationalism," in the *American Historical Review*, vol. xxxii, pp. 719-736 (1926-1927).   The latest discussion of Herder's nationalism is by Ergang, R. R., *Herder and the Foundations of German Nationalism*.

very real sense, the kings anticipated the Republic, and the royal unity was the true source of that one and indivisible unity which became a central tenet of the Revolution.[56] During the seventeenth and eighteeenth centuries, there began to appear, together with this devotion to the king, a conscious loyalty to France itself. Seventeenth-century scholars and men of letters, magistrates and dramatists, men like Chapelain, Voiture, Etienne Pasquier and Corneille, exalted patriotism and the sacrifice of the individual to the state, as it had been practised by the Greek and Latin fathers. Later, Voltaire, La Harpe, Vergniaud, Madame Roland and Camille Desmoulins spoke this same language. The invasion of France during the war of the Spanish Succession prompted an outburst of patriotic devotion to France. Fénelon wrote in 1710: " The king's affairs have become violently our own . . . the nation must save itself." [57] By the middle of the eighteenth century, Fénelon, La Bruyère, Montesquieu, Voltaire and others began to lay emphasis upon the absence of patriotism in France, a defect which they ascribed to the dearth of political liberty. They began to insist upon the necessity of patriotism and to recognize that, to be a true patriot, a man must be an active member of the state.[58] Jean Jacques Rousseau insisted upon the sanctity of the " general will." In his advice to the Polish people he depicted the magic virtues of a conscious loyalty to *la patrie*, the tremendous value of national institutions, especially education, in forming the character and stimulating the patriotism of a people, and he lamented the lack of distinguishing national characteristics in France and the other

---

[56] Stewart and Desjardins, *op. cit.*, p. xii.

[57] Fénelon to the Duc de Chevreuse, 4 Aug., 1710, quoted by Stewart and Desjardins, *op. cit.*, p. xvi.

[58] *Ibid.*, pp. xvi-xxv.

countries of Europe.[59]   The seed of new loyalties was being scattered, and then, with the Revolution, came the germination of French nationalism.

The creation of an elective National Assembly, representative of the French people; the destruction of feudal privilege on the night of 4 August, 1789; the territorial redivision of France, sweeping away jealousies and particularisms of long standing, all these prepared the way for a complete change of allegiance from the king to the nation.   By 1790, Madame Roland and other leaders were asserting that the kingdom of France had become *une patrie*,[60] and succeeding events brought a complete and fanatical allegiance to *la France*.   On 14 July, 1790, was held the first Festival of the Federation, a spontaneous expression of loyalty to a unified nation that existed by the free will of the individuals composing it.   In June, 1791, the king's flight to Varennes marked the beginning of a succession of events that closed, the following year, with his denunciation in the Legislative Assembly as a traitor to the constitution, his deposition, and the declaration of the Republic, One and Indivisible.

Thus, loyalty to person or dynasty was replaced for the majority of Frenchmen by loyalty to an idea.   In the summer and fall of 1792 came, in quick succession, the decree declaring the country in danger, Brunswick's Manifesto, the repulse of the Prussians at Valmy, and then 6 November, the glorious victory of Jemappes.   The French had succeeded in defending their new principles, which were now held to be so sacred that it was necessary to propagate them throughout Europe.   With the coincident worship of French citizenship, militant patriotism found itself full-fledged and arrayed

---

[59] Rousseau, J. J., " Considérations sur la gouvernement de Pologne," *Oeuvres*, vol. ii, pp. 349-351, 356-357, *et passim*.

[60] Aulard, *Patriotisme française*, pp. 236 *et seq*.

against the world.[61]   Then writers like Rabaut identified *la France* with the people of France, who had made a new constitution and established the principles of liberty and equality, and they glorified the nation, asserting that the mass of citizens is the source of all true governmental powers.   Then Carnot stated to his colleagues that, like individuals in the social order, nations are entities in the political order; that sovereignty does not reside in the whole of the human race, but is national; and that France, as a nation, had a right to independence, safety and unity, and the right to preserve its national honor.   Then Danton, in his fiery speeches to the Convention, made the French nation a living, vital thing. " When the country is in danger," he said in his famous speech of 2 September, 1792, " no one can refuse his services without being branded as infamous and a traitor to *la patrie*. The tocsin which now rings will resound throughout all France.   It is not a signal of alarm.   It sounds the charge against the enemies of *la patrie*."   And again: " When a people offers to march on its enemies, it is necessary to decree, without hesitation, the measures that it demands, for it is the national genius that has dictated those measures."   When he glorified the " great French people," capable of suffering all hardships in the name of liberty, he exclaimed: " Such is the character of the Frenchman, formed by four years of revolution.   Homage to thee, oh sublime people. . . ."[62]

As has been shown in this work, the leaders of the Revolution fostered many projects which, directly or indirectly, stimulated the growth of this political, democratic nationalism.   With them, Sieyes played a very real part.   His nationalism, to be sure, was not well-rounded.   He was not willing, as in the case of French territorial acquisitions from Holland, to give any play to the theory of national self-de-

[61] Stewart and Desjardins, *op. cit.*, pp. xxxi-xxxiv, 1-3.
[62] *Ibid.*, pp. 4, 14-17, 27-29, 47-48.   Reprints of sources.

termination; he disregarded traditions prior to 1789 as a factor in stimulating national consciousness; and one is often impressed by a lack of persistency in his projects and by a deficiency in that emotional appeal which is such a large part of the stock in trade of contemporary nationalism. Nevertheless, he was a nationalist.

He believed that a nation is a living entity, possessed of a " will " which it has the right to express; he believed that the French people constitute a nation endowed with individual characteristics, and possessing peculiar excellencies; he sought, by opposing decentralizing tendencies, by his advocacy of universal military training and the subjection of church to state, and by the creation of the départemental system, to bring into existence a unified France, whose people would be conscious of the fact that they were one, a " grand whole; " and he attempted, by these and various other projects for inspiring national pride and loyalty, to stimulate among the citizens, a feeling of paramount devotion to this, their common *patrie*. In all these, he was in accord with other leaders of the Revolution, who had similar aims.[63]

Lastly, his grandiose foreign policy represents the chauvinistic nationalism that is to be detected in the aims of the later Convention and of the Directory. The subjugation of Holland to France, carried through with the backing of the Committee of Public Safety, and enthusiastically accepted by the Convention; the attempt to reduce Spain to a state of vassalage, an attempt wherein Sieyes acted as the chief agent of the Committee of Public Safety; and later, the endeavor to remake the map of Europe in the interest of French supremacy, an endeavor which was in consonance with the aims of Jean DeBry, Talleyrand and the Directory: all these had their foundation in his belief that it was the mission of

[63] *Cf.* Hayes, C. J. H., *The Historical Evolution of Modern Nationalism,* chapter 3, on Jacobin nationalism.

France to obtain and preserve peace, and that peace could only be secured by making France so powerful on the continent that none would dare attack her. This attitude has its replica today in any assembly of extreme nationalists where diplomacy is discussed.

Sieyes was at times, but only at times, a power in political affairs and a leader in the Revolution. He was obstinate, rather morose, terribly opinionated, and these qualities, plus his irritating " infallibility," diminished his popularity and weathered his influences. But, because of his writings and his political activities, he stands out as one of the pioneers in the political, democratic nationalism of the Revolution, and as one of the representatives of the change into the chauvinistic nationalism that is an aspect of the Directorial and Napoleonic period.

Sieyes' remark to Sandoz-Rollin in 1795 bears repetition here, for it furnishes the key to his activities as this work has sought to portray them. " Those who have accused me of being a friend of Austria have lied; those who have represented me as a friend of the Prussians have also lied; I am a Frenchman, and nothing else." He loved his country. He wanted to make it the greatest and the most powerful nation of the earth. His individual efforts to that end were not crowned by any startling triumphs, but his endeavors served to place him among the leaders in fomenting the nationalism of the Revolution, and that was no slight achievement.

BIBLIOGRAPHICAL NOTE

Information as to the youth of Sieyes is scanty and of rather unsatisfactory nature. The student is forced to rely upon the informative but all too scanty reprints of correspondence (Teissier and Neton in *La Nouvelle Revue*) and upon Sainte-Beuve's brilliant and valuable essay in the *Causeries de Lundi*. This essay is based on manuscript and other source material collected some eighty years ago by M. Fortoul, but which has long since disappeared. The above mentioned, together with the *Notice sur la vie*, an apologia that must be carefully handled, and the small amount of help afforded by the archives at Chartres and Orléans, are the main sources for his early life.

Sieyes' work as a pamphleteer is to be studied in the four tracts published during the winter and spring of 1789. Next comes the part that he played in the Revolution. Brette's *Recueil de documents relatifs à la convocation des états généraux de 1789* is indispensable for the foreground. The main sources of information for the period of the Constituant are his writings, practically all of which appeared during 1789-1790 and which are essential and invaluable in studying his career; the *Journal* and *Procès-Verbaux* of the Third Estate and of the National Assembly, which, though good, are sometimes rather barren of detail where it is most needed; the *Archives Parlementaires*, a huge compilation of the proceedings of the Assembly, although sometimes inaccurate; the succinct and valuable *Journal* of Adrien Duquesnoy; and Barère's newspaper, *Le Point du jour*. This latter bears all the evidences of being a careful compilation of the proceedings of the Estates General and the Assembly, but the part dealing with the period from 5 May to the middle of June, 1789, seems to have been made up at a later date and must be used circumspectly. The *Moniteur* began publication in November of '89 and its value increases thereafter, inasmuch as the previous numbers were made up. From the spring of 1790 on, it ranks as a source of great value. Dumont's *Souvenirs* is excellent, but, like all books of its type, must be used cautiously. The best of the memoirs are those of Malouet. Camille Desmoulins' *Révolutions de France et de Brabant* gives tone and sparkle to the period. Camille was a journalist par excellence, a fact to be always kept in mind.

Sieyes drops out of sight with the Legislative Assembly, but returns to a sporadically active part in the Convention and Directory. The *Moniteur*, checked by the procès-verbaux, was my chief reliance in dealing with his relation to domestic affairs during this period. Guillaume's valuable edition of the procès-verbaux of the committee on education in

1793 deserves special mention. For Sieyes' connection with foreign affairs, the documents contained in the *Archives des Affaires Etrangères* and in the *Archives Nationales* are indispensable. In both of these repositories one finds many unpublished letters and manuscripts that throw much light upon his activities while on the Committee of Public Safety and as envoy to Berlin. Along this same line, one may frequently consult Aulard's *Recueil des Actes du Comité de salut public*, and Bailleu's *Preussen und Frankreich von 1795 bis 1807*. The latter is especially valuable for the letters of Sandoz-Rollin, the shrewd Prussian ambassador to Paris. Both are incomplete, especially for purposes of biographical research, and the gaps have to be filled by work in the archives.

There are collections of letters written during this period that are of considerable value. Aside from those of Sandoz-Rollin, there are the shrewd observations of the Baron de Staël-Holstein, ambassador to France from Sweden, and his successor as chargé d'affaires, Baron Brinckman; Humboldt's letters to Schiller, which afford some interesting and valuable comments; and the correspondence of Mallet du Pan with the Viennese court. The latter, written mainly from Berne, seems, nevertheless, to be based on considerable accurate information. The letters of Lafayette are less valuable but still of interest.

The memoirs of the period are to be used with great care. Mainly apologetic, they are also exceedingly inaccurate. I have avoided using them except in cases where they are corroborative or are backed by other supporting evidence.

The study of Sieyes' nationalism is, of course, based upon an intensive analysis of his writings and speeches. These are found in the sources already mentioned, his pamphlets, speeches and correspondence.

For the final years, one again has recourse to the *Moniteur*, and to letters such as those of Brinckman and Mme. Reinhard. Aulard's *Registre des Délibérations du Consulat Provisoire*, and his *Paris sous le Consulat* are valuable collections of documents bearing on this period. The last years, including the exile to Brussels, are best covered by the monograph of Duvivier, which, though padded with extraneous material, is carefully done.

Secondary works are many, and I shall mention only a few. Neton's *Sieyes* is a detailed life, accurate in its presentation of facts but biased in favor of Sieyes in its conclusions. Clapham's *The Abbé Sieyes* is a briefer treatment, and is mainly concerned with his political theories. It is an able piece of work.

The bibliography does not pretend to include all outstanding works on the Revolution. Only those that were actually consulted are included. Of these, Aulard's *Histoire politique de la Révolution française* is excellent for a study of the political movements, and the first four volumes of Sorel's *L'Europe et la Révolution française* for the diplomacy of the period to 1795. Bourgeois' *Manuel historique de politique étrangère* is a brief but excellent study of the diplomacy of the Revolution. Lamartine's *Histoire des Girondins* is old but useful. Guyot's *Le Directoire et la paix de l'Europe* is the best treatment of the foreign policy of the Directory, and Vandal's *L'Avènement de Bonaparte* is the best lengthy treatment of Brumaire and the period following, although favorable to the Corsican. It is particularly valuable for its citation of Cambacérès' *Eclaircissements* and the manuscript note of Grouvelle, the close friend of Sieyes. The former are in a private collection, and the latter, although supposedly in the *Bibliothèque de la ville de Paris*, are at present not available. Mention should also be made of Boulay de la Meurthe's excellent *Théorie constitutionnelle de Sieyes*, which is, to all intents and purposes, next to a source in value, and gives us our best idea of Sieyes' constitutional plans in 1799. There are also some excellent biographies, such as the "Life" of Boulay de la Meurthe, Cahen's *Condorcet*, the life of Louis David by J. L. David, *Thouret* by Lebègue, and others. These are often found to contain valuable material that would otherwise have escaped notice, and their interpretations of given situations are sometimes challenging and generally illuminating.

Special mention should be made of monographs such as Boulay de la Meurthe's *Le Directoire et l'expédition d'Egypte*, Brette's excellent *Limites et divisions territoriales de la France en 1789*, Fromont's *Essai sur l'administration de l'Assemblée provinciale d'Orléans*, and also Sagnac's masterly *Législation civile de la Révolution française*. The best book on the French press is that of Mlle. Soderhjelm, *Le Regime de la presse pendant la Révolution française*, which is a mine of accurate and useful information.

ABBREVIATIONS

Arch. des Aff. Etran. . . . .*Archives des Affaires Etrangères.*
Arch. Nat'l. . . . .*Archives Nationales.*
Arch. Parl. . . . .*Archives Parlementaires.*
Délibérations . . . .*Délibérations à prendre dans les assemblées.*
Fol. . . . .*Folio.*
Notice . . . .*Notice sur la vie de Sieyes.*
Procès-Verbal . . . .*Procès-Verbal de l'Assemblée Nationale.*
Qu'est-ce que . . . .*Qu'est-ce que le tiers état.*
Révol. franç. . . . .*La Révolution française.*

BIBLIOGRAPHY

Bibliographical Aids

Barbier, Ant.-Alex., *Dictionnaire des ouvrages anonymes*. 3rd ed., Paris, Billard, 1872.

Brière, G. et Caron, P., *Repertoire methodique de l'histoire moderne et contemporaine de la France*. Paris, 1896-1912.

Caron, P., *Bibligraphie des travaux publiés de 1866 à 1897 sur l'histoire de France depuis 1789*. Paris, E. Cornély et cie, 1912.

Caron, P., *Manuel pratique pour l'étude de la Révolution française*. Paris, Picard, 1912.

Hatin, L. E., *Bibliographie historique et critique de la presse periodique française*. Paris, Firmin-Didot frères, fils et cie, 1866.

Garrett, M. B., A " Critical Bibliography of the Pamphlet Literature published in France between 5 July and 27 December, 1788," in the *Howard College Bulletin*, April, 1925.

Kircheisen, F. M., *Bibliographie du temps de Napoleon*. Champion, 1908-1912, 2 vols.

Langlois, Ch., *Manuel de bibliographie historique*. Paris, 1896-1904, 2 vols.

Schmidt, Ch., *Les Sources de l'histoire de France aux Archives Nationales*. Paris, 1907.

Tuetey, Alex., *Les Papiers des Assemblées de la Révolution aux Archives Nationales*. Paris, 1908.

Tuetey, Alex., *Publications sur la la Révolution à Paris. Repertoire des sources manuscrites*. Paris, 1890-1910, 11 vols.

Writings of Emmanuel Joseph Sieyes

"Aperçu d'une nouvelle organisation de la justice et de la police en France" in the *Arch. Parl.*, series i, vol. xii, pp. 249-258.

Déclaration des droits de l'homme en société à l'Assemblée Nationale. Versailles, Baudouin, 1789.

Déclaration volontaire proposée aux patriotes des quatre-vingt-trois départements. Paris, June, 1791.

Dire—sur la question du veto royal—a l'Assemblée Nationale. Paris, Sept., 1789.

Instructions donnée par S.A.S. Monseigneur le duc d'Orléans, à ses représentants aux bailliages. Suivie de délibérations à prendre dans des Assemblées. 2e éd., corrigée, Paris, 1789.

Observations sommaires sur les biens ecclésiastiques du 10 août, 1789. Bordeaux, l'imprimerie de Simonde la Court, 1789.

Observations sur le rapport du comité de Constitution concernant la nouvelle organisation de la France. Versailles, Baudouin, 1789.

Opinion de M. l'Abbé Sieyes sur l'arrêté du 4 relatif aux dîmes. Paris, Aug., 1789.

Préliminaire de la constitution; reconnaissance et exposition raisonnée des droits de l'homme et du citoyen. Versailles, Baudouin, 1789.

" Le Projet de traité présenté au Comité de Salut Public par le citoyen Sieyes, membre dubit Comité, en l'an III de la Republic," in the *Archives des Affaires Etrangères, mémoires et documents,* Allemagne 117, folio 29.

Projet d'un décret provisoire sur le clergé. Paris, l'imprimerie Nationale, 1790.

Quelques idées de constitution applicables à la ville de Paris en juillet, 1789. Versailles, Baudouin, 1789.

Qu'est-ce que le tiers état—précédé de l'essai sur les privilèges. E. Champion, ed., Paris, 1888.

Vues sur les moyens d'exécution dont les représentants de la France pourront disposer en 1789. 2e éd., Paris, 1789.

OTHER PRIMARY MATERIALS

Antraigues, Le comte d'., *Mémoire sur les états généraux.* Paris, 1788.

Antraigues, Le comte d'., *Observations sur la nouvelle division du royaume, proposée par le comité de constitution.* Paris, 1789.

Archives des Affaires Etrangères. Correspondance Politique Hollande, Espagne, Prusse, Allemagne; Mémoires et Documents France, Espagne, Allemagne.

Archives d'Eure et Loir. Register, *procès-verbaux* and miscellaneous manuscripts of the départemental assembly of Chartres and Dourdan.

Archives du Loiret. Register, *procès-verbaux* and miscellaneous manuscripts of the provincial assembly of Orléans.

Archives Nationales. Series AFIII, AFIV, C, CC.

Archives parlementaires de 1787-1860. Première série (1789 à 1799) imprimé par ordre de l'Assemblée Nationale sous la direction de M. J. Mavidal . . . et de MM. E. Laurent et E. Clavel. 2e éd., Paris, p. Dupont, 1879-1914, 82 vols.

Aulard, F.-V.-A., *Paris sous le consulat.* Paris, L. Cerf., 1903, 2 vols.

Aulard, F.-V.-A., *Recueil des actes du comité de salut public.* Paris, imprimerie nationale, 1889-1923, 26 vols.

Aulard, F.-V.-A., *Registre des délibérations du Consulat provisoire.* Paris, 1894.

Aulard, F.-V.-A., *La Société des Jacobins.* Paris, Jouaust (etc.), 1889-1897, 6 vols.

Bacourt, A. de., *Correspondance entre le comte de Mirabeau et la Comte de la Marck.* Paris, V. Le Normant, 1851, 3 vols.

Bailleu, P., *Preussen und Frankreich von 1795 bis 1807. Diplomatischen Correspondenzen. Publicationen aus den Preussischen Archiven.* Leipzig, S. Hirzel, 1881-1887, 2 vols.

Barthélemy, François marquis de., *Papiers de Barthélemy, ambassadeur de France en Suisse, 1792-1797.* J. Kaulek et Tausserat Radel eds. Paris, F. Alcan, 1886-1910, 6 vols.

Baudot, M. A., *Notes historiques sur la convention nationale, le directoire, l'empire et l'exil des votants.* Paris, L. Cerf, 1893.

Beaulieu, C. F., *Essais historiques sur les causes et les effets de la révolution de France.* Paris, Maradan, an IX-XI (1801-1803), 6 vols.

Bloch, C., *Cahiers de doléances du bailliage d'Orléans pour les états généraux de 1789.* Orléans, Leroux, 1906-1907, 2 vols.

Brette, A., *Recueil de documents relatifs à la convocation des états généraux de 1789.* Paris, imprimerie nationale, 1894-1904, 3 vols.

Boucher-Laricharderie, G., *De L'Influence de la révolution française sur le caractère national.* Paris, an VI.

Brougham, Henry Lord, *Works.* Edinburgh, 1872, 11 vols.

Bruchstücke aus den Papieren eines Augenzeugen und unparteiischen Beobachters der franzoesischen Revolution. s.l., 1794.

Buchez, P.-J.-B. et Roux, P.-C., *Histoire parlementaire de la révolution française.* Paris, Paulin, 1834-1838, 40 vols.

Cabanis, P.-J.-G., *Oeuvres.* Paris, 1823, 5 vols.

Cabet-Gassicourt, *Le Tombeau de Jacques Molai, ou histoire secrète et abrégée des initiés anciens et modernes des Templiers, Franc-Maçons, Illuminés.* 2e éd., Paris, Desenne, an V.

Cerutti, J., " Mémoire pour le peuple française," in *La Révolution française,* vol. xv, pp. 55-85, July, 1888.

Challamel, A., *Les Clubs contre-révolutionnaires.* Paris, L. Cerf, 1895.

Charavay, E., *Procès-Verbaux de l'assemblée electorale de Paris.* Paris, Jouaust, 1890-, 3 vols.

Chassin, Ch.-L., *Les Elections et les cahiers de Paris en 1789.* Paris, Jouaust et Sigaux, 1888-1889, 4 vols.

Chénier, A., *Oeuvres en prose de André Chénier.* L. Becq de Fauquières, ed. Paris, 1872.

Collège des Grassins, *Liste des élèves de logique et de physique au collège des Grassins de 1767 à 1778.*

Condillac, Etienne de, *Oeuvres.* Paris, Dufart, 1798, 23 vols.

Condorcet, M.-J.-A.-N.-C., *Oeuvres.* A. Condorcet O'Connor and M. F. Arago eds., Paris, 1847-1849, 12 vols.

Constant, B., *Journal Intime.* D. Melegari, ed., Paris, P. Ollendorf, 1895.

Correspondance secrète inédite sur Louis XVI, Marie Antoinette, La Cour et la Ville, de 1777 à 1792. M. de Lescure, ed, Paris, 1866, 2 vols.

Courrier de Provence, Mirabeau and Duroveray, eds., Paris, 2 May, 1789–30 Sept., 1791, 352 nos. in 17 vols.

Debidour, A., *Recueil des actes du Directoire exécutif.* Paris, E. Leroux, 1910, 4 vols.

Desmoulins, Camille, *Oeuvres.* J. Claretie, ed., Paris, E. Plon et cie, 1874, 2 vols.

Dropmore Papers, *Manuscripts of J. B. Fortescue, esq.*, preserved at Dropmore. Published by the Historical Manuscripts Commission, London, 1892-1915, 9 vols.

Duquesnoy, A., *Journal sur l'assemblée constituante, 3 mai, 1789-3 avril, 1790.* Paris, A. Picard et fils, 1894, 2 vols.

Duvergier, J.-B., *Collection complète des lois, décrets, ordonnances, règlemens et avis du Conseil d'Etat . . . de 1788 à 1824.* Paris, 1824-1878, 78 vols.

Examen du "préliminaire de la constitution" de M. l'Abbé Sieyes . . . s. l. n. d.

Faure, P.-J.-D.-G., *Au Représentant Sieyes, sur un projet de constitution.* Paris, de l'Imprimerie Nationale, thermidor, l'an III.

Fauriel, C., *Les Derniers Jours du Consulat.* L. Lalenne, ed., Paris, 1889.

France—Assemblée Nationale Constituante. Journal des Etats Généraux. Le Hodey, ed., Paris, Devaux et Gatty, Le Hodey (etc.), 1789-1791, 35 vols.

France—Assemblée Nationale Constituante. Procès-Verbal de l'Assemblée Nationale. Paris, Baudouin, 1789-1791, 75 vols.

Gazette de Paris, B. F. de Rozoi, ed., Oct., 1789–Aug., 1792, 6 vols..

Girardin, S. de, *Journal et Souvenirs.* Paris, 1828.

Gower, G. G. Leveson, Earl, *The Despatches of Earl Gower.* Browning, O., ed., Cambridge, Royal Historical Society, 1885.

Guffroy, A.-B.-J., *Lettre en reponse aux observations sommaires de M. l'Abbé Sieyes, sur les biens ecclésiastiques.* Paris, 1789.

Hardenberg, C. A. Fursten von, *Denkwürdigkeiten des Staatskanzlers Fürsten von Hardenberg.* L. von Ranke, ed., Leipzig, 1877, 6 vols.

Humboldt, Wm. von, *Neue Briefe Wilhelm von Humboldts an Schiller.* Berlin, Ebrard, 1796-1803.

Journal de la Société de 1789. Condorcet, Du Pont de Nemours (etc.), eds., Paris, Lejay fils, 5 June–15 Sept., 1790, 1 vol.

Journal des hommes libres de tous les pays, ou le Republicain. Paris, 1 er mess.–17 fruc., an VII, 1 vol.

Lenglet, E.-G., *Du Domaine national; ou, réponse à M. l'Abbé Sieyes sur les biens ecclésiastiques.* Paris, 1789.

La Croix, S., *Actes de la commune de Paris pendant la Révolution.* Paris, L. Cerf, 1894-1898, 7 vols.

Locke, J., *An Essay Concerning Human Understanding.* 20th ed., London, T. Longman (etc.), 1796, 2 vols.

Locke, J., *Two Treatises of Government*. 2nd. ed., London, printed for Awnsham and John Churchill, at the Black Swan in Paternoster-Row, 1694.

Mallet du Pan, J., *Correspondance inédite de Mallet du Pan avec la cour de Vienne (1794-1798)*. Paris, E. Plon, Nourrit et cie, 1884, 2 vols.

Mallet du Pan, J., *Mercure Britannique*. Londres, W. and C. Spilsbury, Snow-Hill, 10 Oct., 1798–25 March, 1800, 5 vols. in 4.

Marat, J. P., *La Correspondance de Marat*. Ch. Vellay, ed., Paris, 1908.

Martens, G. F. von, *Recueil des principaux traités . . . conclus par les puissances de l'Europe . . . depuis 1761 jusqu' à présent*. A. Gottingue, J. C. Dieterich, 1791-, 97 vols. to 1920.

Mercy-Argenteau, F.-C., *Correspondance secrète avec l'Empereur Joseph II et le prince de Kaunitz*. D'Arneth et Flammermont, eds., Paris, 1889, 2 vols.

Mirabeau, H.-G., *Oeuvres*. J. Mailhou, ed., Paris, 1834.

Moleville, B. de, *Annals of the French Revolution*. R. C. Dallas, trans., London, 1800, 4 vols.

Monin, H., *L'Etat de Paris en 1789*. Paris, D. Jouaust (etc.), 1889.

Moniteur (Gazette Nationale ou le Moniteur Universel). C. J. Panckoucke, et al., eds., Paris, 1789-1867, 157 vols.

Morris, G., *Journal de Gouverneur Morris*. E. Pariset, trans., Paris, Plon-Nourrit et cie, 1901.

Mounier, J.-J., *Exposé de la conduite de M. Mounier dans l'Assemblée Nationale*. s. l. n. d.

Mousset, A., *Un Témoin ignoré de la Révolution. Le Comte de Fernan Núñez, ambassadeur d'Espagne à Paris (1787-1791)*. Paris, E. Champion, 1923.

Notice sur la vie de Sieyes . . . écrite à Paris. London, Johnson, 1795.

Observateur politique, litteraire et commercial. Geoffroi, ed., Paris, therm., an VI—plur., an VII, 3 vols.

Pallain, G., *Le Ministère de Talleyrand sous le Directoire*. Paris, E. Plon, Nourrit et cie, 1891.

Pierre, V., *18 Fructidor. Documents pour la plupart inédits*. Paris, 1893.

Point du jour, Le Barère de Vieuzac, ed., Paris, Cussac, 19 June, 1789-1 Oct. 1791, nos. 1-815.

Procès-Verbaux du comité d'instruction . . . de la Convention. Guillaume, M. J., ed., Paris Hachette et cie, 1891, 6 vols.

Procès-Verbaux des séances de l'assemblée provinciale de l'orléanais. Orléans, 1787.

Publiciste, Le. Paris, 7 niv., an VI—1 nov., 1810, 37 vols.

Qu'est-ce que le peuple. Paris, Mess., an VII.

Reinhard, Mme. C., *Lettres de Madame Reinhard à sa mère. La Baronne de Wimpffen*, ed., Paris, A. Picard et fils, 1900.

Révolutions de France et de Brabant. C. Desmoulins, ed. (later, Dusaulchoy), Paris, 1789-1791. 104 nos. in 17 vols.

Révolutions de Paris. Prudhomme, Loustalot, etc., eds., Paris, 12 July, 1789-28 Feb., 1794. 225 nos. in 17 vols.

Reynaud, M. Jean, *La Vie et correspondance de Merlin de Thionville.* Paris, Furne et cie, 1860. 2 vols. in one.

Ricard, Le Ch. de, *De la Force publique au dedans et au dehors de l'état; des milices et de l'armée.* Paris, Desenne, 1er Nov., 1789.

Ricard, M., député de Nimes, *Réflexions sur le projet de M. l'Abbé Sieyes, du 12 fevrier dernier, concernant les biens du clergé.* s. l. n. d.

Robespierre, M., *Correspondance de Maximilien et Augustin Robespierre.* G. Michon, ed., Paris, 1926.

Robiquet, P., *Le Personnel municipal de Paris pendant la révolution.* Paris, 1890.

Roederer, P.-L., *Oeuvres du comte P. L. Roederer . . . publié par son fils le baron A.-M. Roederer.* Paris, Firmin Didot frères, 1853-1859, 8 vols.

Roland, Mme., *Lettres de Mme. Roland.* C. Perroud, ed., Paris, 1902, 2 vols.

Roland, Mme., *Lettres en partie inédites de Madame Roland aux demoiselles Cannet, suivies des lettres de Madame Roland à Bosc.* C.-A. Dauban, ed., Paris, 1867, 2 vols.

Rousseau, J. J., *Oeuvres,* vol. ii, Paris, Garnier frères, n. d.

Salamon, l'Abbe de, *Correspondance secrète de l'Abbé de Salamon, chargé des affaires du saint-siege pendant la révolution, avec le Cardinal de Zelada (1791-1792).* Le Vte. de Richemont, ed., Paris, E. Plon, Nourrit et cie, 1898.

Sejour en France de 1792 à 1795, Un. H. Taine, ed., 2nd. ed., Paris, 1872.

Staël, Mme. de, *Des Circonstance actuelles qui peuvent terminer la révolution.* J. Vienot, ed., Paris, 1906.

Staël, Mme. de, *Considerations on the Principal Events of the French Revolution.* Duke de Broglie and Baron de Staël, eds., N. Y., J. Eastburn and Co., 1818, 2 vols.

Staël, Mme. de, *Oeuvres.* Paris, Treuttel et Wurtz, 1820-1821, 19 vols.

Staël-Holstein, E.-M., baron de, *Correspondance diplomatique du Baron de Staël-Holstein, ambassadeur de Suede en France, et de son successeur comme chargé d'affaires, le Baron Brinckman (1783-1799).* L. Leouzon Le Duc, ed., Paris, Hachette et cie, 1881.

Voyez comme on vous égaré. S. l. n. d.

Willerval, M., *Réflexions rapides concernant l'opinion de M. l'Abbé Sieyes sur l'arrêté pris, le 4 Aout, 1789, par l'Assemblée-Nationale, relativement aux dimes.* Paris, 27 Oct., 1789.

William, H. M., *Lettres sur les événemens qui sont passes en France depuis le 31 Mai, 1793, jusqu'au 10 Thermidor.* Paris, s. d.

Young, A., *Travels in France.* 2nd. ed., London, G. Bell and Sons, 1889, 2 vols.

MEMOIRS

Bailly, J.-S., *Mémoires*. Paris, Baudouin frères, 1821-1822, 3 vols.

Barèe de Vieuzac, B., *Mémoires*. Paris, J. Labitte, 1842, 4 vols.

Barras, P.-F.-J.-N., *Mémoires de Barras, membre du Directoire*. G. Duruy, ed., Paris, Hachette et cie, 1895-1896, 4 vols.

Beugnot, Comte, *Mémoires du Comte Beugnot*. Comte Albert Beugnot, ed., Paris, 1889.

Bonaparte, L., *Lucien Bonaparte et ses mémoires*. Th. Jung, ed., Paris, 1882, 3 vols.

Bourrienne, L.-A. F. de, *Mémoires de M. de Bourrienne*. Brussels, 1829, 10 vols.

Brissot de Warville, J. P., *Mémoires*. Cl. Perroud, ed., Paris, A. Picard et fils, 1911, 2 vols.

Cornet, M.-A., Cte., *Notice sur le 18 Brumaire*. S. l. n. d.

Dumont, E., *Souvenirs sur Mirabeau et sur les deux premières assemblées législatives*. Paris, C. Gosselin et chez H. Bossange, 1832.

Fauche Borel, M. Louis, *Précis Historique*. Paris, October, 1815.

Ferrières, C.-E. Marquis de, *Mémoires du Marquis de Ferrières*. Paris, 1822, 3 vols.

Fouché, J., *Mémoires de Joseph Fouché, Duc d'Otrante*. Paris, chez Le Rouge, 1824, 2 vols.

Gaëte, M.-M.-C.-G., *Mémoires, souvenirs, opinions et écrits du Duc de Gaëte*. Paris, Baudouin frères, 1826, 2 vols.

Gohier, L. J., *Mémoires*. Paris, 1824, 2 vols.

Gourgaud, G. General Baron, *Sainte Hélène. Journal inédit de 1815 à 1818*. 3rd. ed., Paris, E. Flammarion, 1899, 2 vols.

Grégoire, H., *Mémoires de Grégoire*. M. H. Carnot, ed., Paris, 1840, 2 vols.

Jourdan, Marechal, " Notice sur le 18 brumaire," in the *Carnet Historique*, vol. vii, pp. 161-172, Feb., 1901.

Lafayette, M.-J. Marquis de, *Mémoires, correspondance et manuscrits du General Lafayette, publiés par sa famille*. Paris, H. Fournier ainé, 1837-1838, 6 vols.

Larevellière-Lépeaux, L. M. de, *Mémoires de Larevellière-Lépeaux*. O. de Larevellière-Lépeaux ed., Paris, E. Plon, Nourrit et cie, 1895, 3 vols.

Las Cases, M.-J. le Comte de, *Journal de la vie privée et des conversations de l'Empereur Napoleon à Sainte Hélène*. *Stockholm*, 1823-1824, 8 vols.

Lavalette, A.-M. Comte de, *Memoirs*. London, 1831, 2 vols.

Macdonald, A., *Souvenirs de Marechal Macdonald*. Paris, 1892, 2 vols.

Mallane, Durand de, *Mémoires sur la Convention Nationale*. M. de Lescure ed., Paris, 1881.

Mallet du Pan, J., *Memoirs and Correspondance.* A Sayous, ed., London, R. Bentley, 1852, 2 vols.

Mallouet, P.-V., *Mémoires.* Paris, E. Plon et cie, 1874, 2 vols.

Napoleon Bonaparte, *Memoirs of the History of France.* Gourgaud and Montholon eds., London, H. Colburn & Co., 1823-1824, 3 vols.

Pasquier, E.-D. le Chancelier, *Mémoires du Chancelier Pasquier.* M. le Duc d'Audiffret-Pasquier ed., Paris, E. Plon, Nourrit et cie, 1894-1896, 6 vols.

Romilly, S., *The Life of Sir Samuel Romilly, written by Himself.* London, 1842, 2 vols.

Rovigo, R. Savary, Duc de, *Mémoires du Duc de Rovigo.* Paris, 1828, 8 vols.

Talleyrand-Perigord, C.-M. le Prince de, *Mémoires du Prince de Talleyrand.* Le Duc de Broglie ed., Paris, Calmann Levy, 1891-1892, 5 vols.

SECONDARY MATERIALS

Acton, J. E. E. D., *Lectures on the French Revolution.* J. N. Figgis and R. V. Laurence eds,, London, 1925.

Aulard, F.-V.-A., *Christianity and the French Revolution.* Lady Fraser, trans., London, Benn, 1927.

Aulard, F.-V.-A., *Etudes et leçons.* Paris, F. Alcan, 1901, 7 vols.

Aulard, F.-V.-A., *Histoire politique de la révolution française.* Paris, A. Colin, 1901.

Aulard, F.-V.-A., *Les Orateurs de l'Assemblée Constituante.* Paris, 1882.

Aulard, F.-V.-A., *Les Orateurs de la Législatif et de la Convention.* Paris, 1886, 2 vols.

Aulard, F.-V.-A., *Le Patriotisme française.* Paris, E. Chiron, 1921.

Aulard, F.-V.-A., " Le Serment du jeu de paume," in *La Révolution française,* vol xvii, pp. 7-19, July, 1889.

Aulard, F.-V.-A., " Sieyes et Talleyrand, d'après Benjamin Constant et Barras," in *La Révolution française,* vol. lxxiii, pp. 289-314, Nov., 1920.

Barker, E., *National Character.* London, Methuen & Co., ltd., 1927.

Beauverger, E. de, *Tableau historique des progrès de la philosophie politique.* Paris, 1858.

Bethouart, A., *Histoire de Chartres.* Chartres, 1903, 2 vols.

Bluntschli, J. K., *Geschichte der Neureren Staatswissenschaft, Allgemeines Staatsrecht und Politik.* Dritte Auflage, Munchen und Leipzig, 1881.

Boisllaigue, R., *Le Silencieux Sieyes.* Chartres, 1928.

Bonaparte, L., *La Vérité sur les Cent-Jours.* Paris, chez Ladvocat, 1835.

Bonnet, Chas., *Contemplation de la nature.* S. l. n. d.

Boulay de la Meurthe, *Boulay de la Meurthe.* Paris, private printing, 1868.

Boulay de la Meurthe, *Le Directoire et l'expédition d'Egypte*. Paris, Hachette et cie, 1885.

Boulay de la Meurthe, A.-J.-C.-J., *Théorie constitutionnelle de Sieyes*. Paris, 1836.

Bourgeois, E., *Manuel historique de politique étrangère*. Paris, Belin frères, 1901-, 3 vols.

Brandt, O., "Untersuchungen zu Sieyes," in *Historische Zeitschrift*, vol. 126, pp. 410-428, 1922.

Brette, A., *Les Limites et les divisions territoriales de la France en 1789*. Paris, E. Cornély et cie, 1907.

Brette, A., "La Séance royale du 23 juin, 1789", in *La Révolution française*, vol. xxii, pp. 5-44, 120-155, 416, 452, Jan., Feb., May, 1892, and vol. xxiii, pp. 55-76, July, 1892.

Cahen, L., *Condorcet et la révolution française*. Paris, F. Alcan, 1904.

Caraman, Le Duc de, *Charles Bonnet*. Paris, 1859.

Champion, E., "Le Conversion du Comte d'Antraigues," in *La Révolution française*, vol. xxvi, pp. 15-25, Jan., 1894.

Champion, E., *La France d'après les cahiers de 1789*. 2nd. ed., Paris, A. Colin, 1904.

Clapham, J. H., *The Abbe Sieyes; an Essay in the Politics of the French Revolution*. London, P. S. King & Son, 1912.

Clapham, J. H., "A Royalist Spy during the Reign of Terror," in the *English Historical Review*, vol. xii, pp. 67-84, Jan., 1897.

Colfavru, J.-C., "L'Institution du jury en matière civile," in *La Révolution française*, vol. i, pp. 449-477, March, 1881.

Comte, Chas., *Histoire de la garde nationale de Paris*. Paris, 1827.

David, J.-L., *Le Peintre Louis David, 1748-1825*. Paris, 1880-1882, 2 vols.

Deschamps, N., *Les Sociétés secrètes et la société*. 3rd. ed., Paris, 1881.

Desjardins, A., *Sieyes et le jury en matière civile*. Aix, A. Durand et P. Lauriel, 1869.

Dunning, W. A., *A History of Political Theory from Rousseau to Spencer*. N. Y., The Macmillan Co., 1920.

Duvivier, P., *L'Exil du Comte Sieyes à Bruxelles (1816-1830)*. Malines, 1910.

Ergang, R. R., *Herder and the Foundations of German Nationalism*. N. Y., Columbia University Press, 1931.

Fromont, H., Université de Paris. Faculté de droit. *Essai sur l'administration de l'assemblée provinciale d'Orléans (1787-1790)*. Paris, 1907.

Garrett, M. B., "The Pamphlet Crisis in France in 1789," in the *Howard College Bulletin*, June, 1927.

Grimaux, E., *Lavoisier, 1743-1794*. 3rd. ed., Paris, F. Alcan, 1899.

Guyot, R., *Le Directoire et la paix de l'Europe*. Paris, F. Alcan, 1912.

Haller, C. L. von, *Restauration der Staatswissenschaft*. 2nd. ed., Winterthur, 1820-1825, 6 vols.

Hatin, L. E., *Histoire politique et litteraire de la presse en France.* Paris, Poulet, Malassis et De Broise, 1859-1861, 8 vols.

Hayes, C. J. H., " Contributions of Herder to the Doctrines of Nationalism," in the *American Historical Review,* vol. xxxii, pp. 719-736, 1926-1927.

Hayes, C. J. H., *Essays on Nationalism.* N. Y., The Macmillan Co., 1926.

Hayes, C. J. H., "The Philosopher Turned Patriot," in *Essays in Intellectual History,* Harper & Bros., 1929.

Hayes, C. J. H., *Historical Evolution of Modern Nationalism.* N. Y., R. R. Smith, 1931.

Iung, Th., *Dubois-Crancé.* Paris, Charpentier, 1884, 2 vols.

Lamartine, A. de, *Histoire des Girondins.* 3rd. ed., Paris, Furne, etc., 1848, 8 vols.

Lanfrey, P., *The History of Napoleon the First.* 3rd. ed., N. Y. and London, Macmillan and Co., 1894, 4 vols.

Lebègue, E., *La Vie et l'oeuvre d'un constituant—Thouret.* Paris, F. Alcan, 1910.

Lavisse, E., *Histoire de France.* Paris, 1911, 18 vols. in 9.

Mege, F., *Gaultier de Biauzat . . . sa vie et sa correspondance.* Clermont-Ferrand, Bellot et fils, 1890, 2 vols.

Merlin, R., *Merlin de Thionville.* Paris, F. Alcan, 1927, 2 vols.

Mignet, M., *Portraits et notices histoqiques.* 3rd. ed., Paris, Charpentier, 1854, 2 vols.

Neton, A. H., " Les Débuts de Sieyes," in *La Nouvelle Revue,* new series, vol. i, pp. 576-588, Dec., 1899.

Neton, A. H., *Sieyes (1748-1836).* Paris, Perrin et cie, 1900.

Oelsner, K. E., *Des Opinions politiques du citoyen Sieyes.* Paris, Gaujon, an VIII.

Reisner, E. H., *Nationalism and Education since 1789.* N. Y., The Macmillan Co., 1922.

Renouvin, P., *Les Assemblées provinciales de 1787.* Paris, A. Picard, 1921.

Robinet, J.-F.-E., *Condorcet, sa vie, son oeuvre.* Paris, Libraries-Imprimeries Réunies, s. d.

Robinet, J.-F.-E., *Danton, homme d'état.* Paris, 1889.

Robinet, J.-F.-E., *Le Mouvement réligieux à Paris pendant la révolution.* Paris, L. Cerf, etc., 1896-1898, 2 vols.

Robiquet, P., *Le Personnel municipal de Paris pendant la révolution.* Paris, D. Jouaust, etc., 1890.

Sagnac, P., *La Législation civile de la révolution française.* Paris, Hachette et cie, 1898.

Sainte-Beuve, C. A. de, *Causeries du lundi.* Paris, Garnier frères, 1852-1862, 15 vols.

Saint-Martin, J., " Un Attentat contre Sieyes," in *La Révolution française,* vol. i, pp. 221-232, March, 1906.

Schaffner, S., *Die Sieyes'schen Enthwürfe und die Entstehung der Verfassung des Jahres VIII.* Leipzig, 1907.

Soderhjelm, A., *Le Regime de la presse pendant le révolution française.* Helsingfors, Imprimerie Hufvudstadsbladet, 1900-1901, 2 vols.

Sorel, A., " L'Autriche ' et le Comité de Salut Public," in the *Revue Historique,* vol. xvii, pp. 25-63, Sept., 1881.

Sorel, A., " Le Comité de Salut Public et la question de la rive gauche du Rhin," in the *Revue Historique,* vol. xviii, pp. 273-322, April, 1882.

Sorel, A., *L'Europe et la révolution française.* Paris, E. Plon, Nourrit, et cie, 1901-, 8 vols.

Sorel, A., " Les Frontières constitutionnelles, 1795," in the *Revue Historique,* vol. xix, pp. 21-59, May, 1882.

Sparks, J., *The Life of Gouverneur Morris.* Boston, Gray and Rowen, 1832, 3 vols.

Stephens, H. M., *A History of the French Revolution.* N. Y., 1886, 3 vols.

Stern, A., " Sieyes et la constitution de 1795," in *La Révolution française,* vol. xxxix, pp. 375-379, Oct., 1900.

Sybel, H. von, *Geschichte der Revolutionszeit.* Stuttgart, 1879, 5 vols.

Taillandier, A.-H., *Documents biographiques sur Danou.* Paris, 1841.

Teissier, O., " La Jeunesse de l'Abbé Sieyes," in *La Nouvelle Revue,* vol. cix, pp. 128-146, Nov., 1897.

Thénard, J., " L'Abbé Sieyes électeur et élu, 1789," in *La Révolution française,* vol. xiv, pp. 1083-1089, June, 1888.

Tissot, M.-P.-F., *Histoire complète de la révolution.* Paris, 1834-1837, 6 vols.

Vandal, A., *L'Avènement de Bonaparte.* Paris, Plon, Nourrit, et cie, 1903-1907, 2 vols.

Vandal, A., " Brumaire," in *Le Correspondant,* 10, 25 Nov., 10 Dec., 1900.

Vandal, A., " Les Causes directes du dix-huit brumaire," in the *Revue des Deux Mondes,* 1, 15 April, 1 May, 1900.

Vialay, A., *Les Cahiers de doléances du tiers état aux états général en 1789.* Paris, 1911.

Vialles, P., *L'Archichancelier Cambacérès* (1753-1824). Paris, 1908.

Welvert, E., " Les Conventionnels régicides après la révolution," in the *Revue Historique,* vol. lxiv, pp. 298-326, May-Aug., 1897.

INDEX

169